STRONGER Families, STRONGER Communities

20 Years of Highly Effective Teaching Practices Supporting Two-Generation Learning

Authored By

Kim Jacobs

National Center for Families Learning

Presented by

TOYOTA

STRONGER FAMILIES STRONGER COMMUNITIES –
20 Years of highly effective teaching practices supporting two-generation learning
© 2016 National Center for Families Learning. All rights reserved. Printed in the United States of America. No part of this book may be used or reproduced in any manner whatsoever without written permission except in the case of brief quotations embodied in critical articles and reviews. For information address National Center for Families Learning, 325 West Main Street, Suite 300, Louisville, KY 40202.

familieslearning.org

First Edition

ISBN - 978-0-692-77751-0

NCFL is grateful for the support and input from the 20 *Toyota Teachers of the Year* who have contributed to this publication. This book is about you, and for you, but most importantly, it is from you. It is your contribution to the field of families learning together.

Thank you for sharing.

Contents

A Message from the President 1

Section 1

Introduction 5

Highly Effective Practices of Family Learning Teachers—
   From Teacher to Teacher 7

Evolution of Family Engagement...19

Section 2

The Toyota Family Teacher of the Year Award—
   Historical Perspective 25

Introduction to the Toyota Family Teacher of the Year Profiles 29

Toyota Family Teacher of the Year Profiles 30

    2016 – Jean Ciborowski Fahey (Weymouth, Massachusetts) 30

    2015 – Kristen Whitaker (Washington, D.C.)...34

    2014 – Elizabeth Atack (Nashville, Tennessee) 38

    2013 – Carolyn Blocker (Long Beach, California) 43

    2012 – Shari Brown (Caldwell County, North Carolina) 46

    2011 – Patricia Urdialez (Mesa, Arizona) 50

    2010 – Karen Kay Brown (Bernice, Louisiana) 54

    2009 – María Antonia Piñón (Miami, Florida)..58

    2008 – Katy Kibbey (Hamtramck, Michigan) 62

    2007 – Gretchen Conway (Lenoir, North Carolina) 67

    2006 – Mark Faloni (Washington, D.C.) 70

    2005 – Amy Hall (Wilson, Michigan) 74

    2004 – Lorie Preheim (Washington, D.C.) 78

    2003 – Jody Lintzenich (Nashville, Tennessee)...82

    2002 – Gwendolyn Paul (Coolidge, Arizona) 86

    2001 – Cecilia Ramirez (Tucson, Arizona) 89

    2000 – Sharonrose McMarr-Schroeder (Los Angeles, California) 93

    1999 – Dayle Bailey (Rockingham, North Carolina) 94

    1998 – Anita Koch (Belle Glade, Florida)...97

    1997   Karen Klima-Thomas (Mesa, Arizona) 98

Section 3

Introduction 103

Program Information and Teacher Biographies..104

A Message from the President
National Center for Families Learning

For the past 20 years, Toyota has supported the National Center for Families Learning in a national search for outstanding teachers who excel in engaging parents and children together in educational settings. Thousands of families across the United States have benefitted from these teachers—strengthening homes, schools, and communities along the way.

The stories of these teachers and their excellent work have long been noted by NCFL through the hundreds of nominations for the *Toyota Family Teacher of the Year Award*. This book is about the winners of this award, and you will learn not only about their teaching skills, but also about the daily practices that shine a bright light on what high-quality family engagement in education really means. And you will learn about the differences these teachers make for families, programs, schools, and our nation—for all of us.

As we celebrate the 20-year milestone for this award, we also celebrate NCFL's 25-year partnership with Toyota—a collaboration responsible for close to 300 family engagement initiatives established across the nation. As an organization, we are committed to providing educational opportunities for families, particularly families with low literacy and language skills, living in poverty. Teachers recognized through the *Toyota Family Teacher of the Year Award* are also committed to working with these families.

The NCFL-Toyota partnership's commitment to families in need—serving two generations at a time—has made an indelible impact. We gratefully acknowledge Toyota's incredible partnership and applaud its commitment to families.

And, we extend our congratulations to the 20 winners, the runners-up, the finalists, and the many other unheralded, yet tirelessly dedicated, educators who are committed to true family engagement in education. Their work has had an exponential effect on educators, entire communities, and families across the nation. With this publication, it is our intent to amplify that impact even more.

Sharon Darling, President and Founder
National Center for Families Learning

Section One

INTRODUCTION

As a teacher working with children and parents, have you ever wished you could sit down with those who came before you and ask them the nitpicky questions about their careers and teaching practices that would help make a difference in your own teaching career?

Have you ever wondered how they begin and end their days? What they make a point to do each and every day? How they keep their motivation high, year after year?

What lessons learned would they share?

What habits did they develop?

What would they do differently, if given the chance?

Wouldn't the answers to all of these questions, and others, be good information for all new teachers working with families and for experienced teachers alike?

Although we can't pick the brains of every experienced teacher out there, we did have the opportunity to interview and discuss these kinds of topics with the top family learning teachers in the nation. We've picked their brains for you.

In this publication, you will hear from the teacher who said, "I take a full cup of empathy with me to school every day," and why she thinks that is important. And the one who says, "I check my first impressions of parents at the door," and why she looks past her own emotions, to respectfully engage with the parent.

You'll hear from teachers who talk about the importance of building trust, in order to build community within their classrooms—and they will tell you how they did just that.

You'll also hear from the teacher who said, "No child or parent is a cookie cutter. Support each person individually. Remembering this allows you to stay fresh and grow as an educator." And the one who shared with us that, "Negative behavior is an opportunity to remind ourselves that children and adults walk in the door every day with challenges. Be part of their successes."

Not to mention the teacher who urged us to remember that, "All parents want the best for their children," no matter what.

There are many pearls of wisdom that teachers echoed throughout their interviews, such as

- Be positive!
- Meet parents where they are.
- Listen between the lines.
- Make a personal connection, every day, with every student.
- Advocate for families—collect their stories.
- Be honest and real with students.
- Find the humor in everyday life.
- Read, read, read.

But the information doesn't stop there. The teacher profiles provided in this publication share insight into the teachers' viewpoints, philosophies of teaching, and their daily motivation.

These teachers reflected on their practices and were eager to share—like the teacher who reminded us to, "Be very thoughtful when working with families. Keep in mind their vast range of experiences."

And keeping in mind the vast range of experiences that each of the 20 *Toyota Family Teachers of the Year* have under their belts, we present you with their stories.

WHY WRITE THIS BOOK?

The National Center for Families Learning (NCFL) knew that 20 years of scouring the nation for the top teachers of family learning programs had more to offer than simply presenting an award. Each of these award-winning teachers had a story to tell, lessons learned to share, and daily practices and habits to contribute. NCFL also knew that creating a publication to share these insights from teachers with their family learning peers—providing both success stories and sometimes even failures—would greatly contribute to the field of family literacy and family learning.

A goal of this publication was to pull together the most salient information from these award-winning teachers to share with others who work in the field of family learning. We gathered their thoughts, ideas, and statements from interviews, questionnaires, focus groups, and nomination packets to inform our work. The expertise, knowledge, and practical experience of each teacher varied, but many of their common practices were similar. Their lessons learned may not have provided us with definitive insight into what works, and what doesn't work—but perhaps more importantly, what worked for them.

Attempts to contact all 20 teachers were made, and all were invited to participate in this project. One teacher was not located. Teacher profiles were created for all 20 teachers who received the award—with some having more in-depth information than others. Phone interviews and/or the opportunity to complete detailed questionnaires were provided to 19 of the 20 teachers. Five of the teachers participated in a focus group at the 2015 Families Learning Summit.

This year, 2016, marks the 20th year for the *Toyota Family Teacher of the Year award* for highlighting excellence in family engagement in education. What better year than now to showcase these 20 teachers and present their best practices to the field of family learning?

HIGHLY EFFECTIVE PRACTICES OF FAMILY LEARNING TEACHERS

―――――――――――

From Teacher to Teacher

What were the most prevalent common denominators of practices and habits shared by the *Toyota Family Teacher of the Year* award recipients?

A firm commitment to families and a strong work ethic notwithstanding, the award-winning teachers you are about to hear from shared some unique and sometimes not-so-unique approaches to teaching. All teachers are dedicated to their profession at some level and strive to meet the needs and goals of their students and families—but the hard work, effort, dedication, and determination of each of these *Toyota Family Teacher of the Year* recipients go well beyond the basic tasks of teaching in order to best support families, and help them succeed at life. These teachers worked long hours, often taking their support of families outside of the classroom walls and into families' homes and personal lives—sometimes sacrificing time with their own children and families. Most importantly, the teachers taught, but they personalized their teaching to each student. They shared, and they gave of themselves. They showed up, each and every day, and never settled for giving their students less than what they deserved.

This chapter dives deeper into the common practices of the 20 teachers featured in this publication, highlighting the *10 most highly effective practices of family learning teachers*. Those practices are:

Focus on Families
Create Passion and Energy
Build Trust
Build Community
Make Personal Connections/Develop Relationships
Value Teamwork
Be a Learner
Be a Reader
Starting the Day
Ending the Day

Focus on Families

It's not surprising that the most often mentioned subject of the teachers was families. After all, families learning together is the main focus of their teaching. Putting families in the forefront of everything teachers do grounds the teachers in the reality of their jobs—and these 20 teachers are no exception.

One of the strongest statements about family and family literacy came from adult education teacher, Cecilia Ramirez of Tucson, Arizona. She said, "Family literacy is more than a program, it's a value." Putting that into the context of family, she added, "This value is something we transfer to parents, and parents transfer to their children, because the heart of family literacy is the parent and child working together, with mutual learning for the future, to accomplish their goals. It's powerful. When we, the teachers, are able to teach a technique or strategy, we transfer the value to the parents, so they can internalize it, and then transfer that skill to their children."

That, is the true essence of family literacy and family learning. But teachers know there is so much more to understanding families. The award teachers remind us of the strengths of families, and how families bring vast experiences to the classroom community. The teachers share that families are the center of family learning programs, and to keep that center strong, it must be nurtured. Strong centers make strong programs. The teachers encourage treating families like family, advocating for families, and putting themselves in their families' shoes. They advise making parents and families comfortable when they come to school and keeping in touch with them when they do not. The teachers feel it is important to help parents foster a sense of self-efficacy, so they feel successful as their child's first teacher.

Emphasizing that parents are the experts on their own children—not the teachers or staff in the program—was an important focus for all. The teachers remind us that all families love their children and want the best for them—and that when families come to school, teachers need to focus on them, and not their own personal issues, crises, or struggles.

A lesson learned from one teacher that is worth mentioning is to never assume that parents or families don't care about their children's education, or are not interested in learning together as a family. That is often not the case. Many times parents simply do not know how to help their children. Meeting parents where they are and helping take them to the next level, fosters their faith and trust in teachers and programs, but also helps them see the value of their own work with their children.

Families generally value the relationships they have with teachers and schools. Parents in family learning programs want a better life for their children and believe that education is the key. They come to family learning programs for that key to a better life—and they rely on teachers to be there for them and to grow with them, every day. Parents come to family learning programs because they want that better life for their children. They want teachers to help them set goals and provide them with strategies to achieve them.

From teacher to teacher—*put families in the forefront of everything you do.*

Passion and Energy

Part of putting families in the forefront and keeping them engaged may have to do with the passion and energy level of the teacher. Several supervisors or directors of the award-winning teachers mentioned the levels of *Passion and Energy* exerted by the teachers on a daily basis.

Teachers mentioned they felt it was important to see challenge as an opportunity. Addressing that opportunity in an energetic way can help to ease the challenge. Early childhood teacher Amy Hall of Wilson, Michigan, shared, "When I see a negative behavior, it is an opportunity to remind myself that children and adults walk in the door each day with different challenges. I want to be part of their successes." For Amy, that meant putting forth the energy necessary to help that family succeed. Whether arriving at school early to prepare, visiting families at home and delivering activities and homework packets, checking to make sure families are okay, or transporting them to school or events—Amy puts the energy into her families, every single day. In turn, that energy manifests itself into a noticeable passion for her work.

Similarly, Pat Urdialez of Mesa, Arizona, added, "When my students share their successes with me, it gives me more energy and more passion to do even more." She continued with, "I believe in the impact that I have on them. If I show them energy and passion, it will come right back to me in their desire to learn, and in the effort they put forth. I think this is one of the reasons why my classes are well attended and successful."

Being positive and always using a positive approach with families was also frequently mentioned. Lorie Preheim of Washington, DC, shared that she makes it a habit to use a positive approach. "By looking for the good in everything, whether it be people, staff's talents, materials, professional development, and seeing how that can support and improve the work, you create a positive environment with continuous program improvement."

Rather than telling parents about all the wrong things they're doing, Liz Atack of the Nashville Public Library, says positivity is the way to go. She offers parents tips and ideas and explains why they are a good thing. "Often, parents are already doing some of these things (talking with or singing to their children, for example), and giving them encouragement to trust their instincts and go with what they know is very empowering for them."

> ***From teacher to teacher***—*be passionate, enthusiastic, and positive. Love what you do, get out of your comfort zone, and enjoy the experience.*

Build Trust

When teachers share parts of themselves—perhaps not unlike their passion for their jobs and undying energy—families begin to trust. Not all families come to school or programs with a high level of trust for the people conducting the program. A level of trust is something that builds over time.

To *Build Trust* is to nurture learning. Trust grows out of knowing that teachers and program providers are sincere and passionate about what they are doing—and that the student's contributions are also valued. The award teachers talked about building trust as a critical element when working with families. Without some minimal level of trust, not much else happens in the classroom.

Several teachers shared that they make a conscience effort, every day, to enhance the self-esteem of and build confidence in their students and families. They work to make sure that students know they are valued, and that their contributions are welcome and also valued, every day.

Two basic strategies for building trust were mentioned repeatedly—open communication and listening. Gwen Paul of Coolidge, Arizona, thinks it is critically important to be open with parents. "I think there always has to be that open communication with parents, whether the message is good or bad. They have to know we're here for them, because we are working with their children."

Carolyn Blocker from Long Beach, California, talks about listening between the lines. "Listen between the lines to what someone is really trying to tell you. The more you understand the situation, the more you can be helpful." And the more helpful you can be, the more you can gain that student's trust. Gretchen Conway from Lenoir, North Carolina, added that it is important to take time to listen to parents. "I feel like I am a better person and educator by listening more to my parents and judging less." Jean Ciborowski Fahey of Weymouth, Massachusetts says, "The greatest lesson I learned from families is to listen to them."

A veteran teacher of adult ESL students, Mark Faloni of Washington, DC, shared that trust is also comfort. "Having been here so long lends itself to a trust and rapport that I can build with the new students, who find out that I have been doing this for all these years. This experience is comforting to them and they learn to trust that I have their best interests at heart."

The students not only learn to trust the teacher and staff, but also each other. Mark added that in his program, building trust among the classmates is powerful. "Next thing you know," he said, "a parent in the class is now the PTA president. To me, that's the biggest thing—the confidence level and the sharing in class, so that people get friends and classmates. People they can trust." Additionally, when the trust level is high enough, the students feel comfortable sharing many issues with each other. "To me, that's when the trust is so high they've decided, 'I'm going to tell you this.'"

Building trust is about all of these things and more. It's also closely related to building community. For many, it's difficult to build community without first firmly establishing trust. And perhaps, for others, it works in the opposite direction.

> ***From teacher to teacher***—*make sure that students know they are valued, and that their contributions are welcome. Building trust grows out of knowing that teachers are sincere.*

Build Community

We all need a community of support. We all benefit from a community bonded with similar goals and experiences. We are stronger together than separate. These are three strong pieces of advice from teachers regarding community building.

In order to *Build Community*, Amy Hall says you need to create community. In other words, teachers need to do things in order for it to happen. "You create a community where you build trust," she says. "Then step back and it happens." The close relationship between building trust and building community cannot be denied.

To create community is also to create learning partnerships with families and a safe learning environment for them. To do this, Lorie Preheim felt it was important for teachers to teach from their own personal experiences. "…the most powerful learning environment happens when we as teachers share from our personal experiences and talk about our struggles, insights, and successes as parents, workers, community members, and ourselves. When you share your own difficulties, it allows for a more open conversation where the adult students don't feel judged. Students learn that it is okay to make mistakes, and it is okay to try something and have it not work."

María Antonia Piñón of Mesa, Arizona, talked about the importance of including yourself as part of the classroom community. "Be open to being part of the community. Let your guard down and be open to the experience. Be a part of your families' communities."

Collectively, the teachers shared advice about how to build community. Some felt strongly that families and adult students should be involved in most aspects of program planning. Involvement often turns into engagement, and once engaged, communities form and flourish.

Several teachers mentioned the power of home visiting, where the teacher not only gets to learn more about the students and families on their own turf, but is accepted into the home community of the family. This powerful home-school connection has worked successfully at many levels—with preschool-age children through high schoolers.

Some daily practices the teachers felt contributed directly to community building include

- Working together to find solutions to make things better.
- Treating everyone equally and with respect.
- Being kind.
- Not judging.
- Avoiding "you" statements.
- Being genuine, fair and honest with students.
- Avoiding getting mad or upset, but being truthful.
- Finding the humor in everyday life.

Several teachers shared strategies for being inclusive of adult students and creating a strong learning partnership, or community. These include

- Creating roles and responsibilities within the community.
- Forming committees and councils for various ideas and agendas.
- Incorporating buddy systems for learning and social activities.
- Creating routines and rituals unique to the classroom.

Many of these ideas can be carried over into children's classrooms or programs, with the hope that parents and families can also carry them into their homes and into their home communities. When successfully formed, the classroom community grows beyond its four walls to the greater school and eventually into the larger neighborhood community. Partnerships with community agencies then become important with parent involvement encouraged. Build collaborations and partnerships locally, and consider how to support families as they participate in these community partnerships. Many families build a sense of pride when they give back to their home community.

Kay Brown of Bernice, Louisiana, said, "Paying it forward is equipping my participants [families] for a better life that will improve our community, too. Any educators in rural centers like mine can learn how to strengthen their community through the same commitment—to focus not just on this program year, but also on all of the future benefits possible."

> ***From teacher to teacher***—*we all benefit from a community of support. We are stronger together than separate.*

Make Personal Connections and Develop Relationships

Along with the two previously discussed practices, *Build Trust* and *Build Community*, comes the often-mentioned practices of how to *Make Personal Connections and Develop Relationships*. In the words of Dr. James Comer, Professor of Child Psychiatry at Yale University, "No significant learning occurs without a significant relationship," and the teachers agreed that relationships are key.

"If you do not first make a personal connection with your students and allow time for a relationship, they will not trust you with their educational and personal pursuits." Shari Brown of North Carolina discovered that in order to be a successful family literacy instructor, she had to provide her students with a comfortable, accepting learning environment. "Every day I interact with and listen intently to my students and learn from their individual perspectives and life experiences. Having that connection with my students allows me to use their interests and needs as a foundation for my lesson and teach in a holistic manner." She added that, "The ultimate reward is seeing my students succeed in life. When they share their successes and challenges with me, I realize that not only do they hold a special place in my heart, but I hold a special place in their lives also."

Nearly all of the award teachers talked about the importance of making personal connections and developing relationships with their families—or demonstrated the importance of relationships by how they do their day-to-day work. Amy Hall is the first of her staff members to arrive at school each day. She comes in early, with one basic purpose in mind—to make sure she greets each child and parent upon arrival. In the words of Katy Kibbey from Hamtramck, Michigan, "Nothing is more important than the relationship." Making that personal, one-to-one connection, every day, leads directly to the cultivation of the relationship. Katy also shared that although relationships often just develop, most times teachers must be intentional. "You have to show that you're trustworthy, that you're credible, that you're true to your word."

Patricia Urdialez thinks it is important to *invite* students and families into the relationship. She said, "I invite my students into a relationship with family literacy, with me, and with each other—a community bonded with similar goals and experiences. Students are encouraged to come to my room at any time to discuss ideas, plans, and concerns. I engage students with vibrant examples and stories, usually personal. This allows my students to feel comfortable and participate."

Making a personal connection every day was a habit for Cecilia Ramirez. She used the attendance-taking time each morning to focus on individual students—even the ones who were absent. She would ask her students, "'Have you heard anything about this person today?' The point was concern and caring, and for them to develop a deeper understanding of the value of school attendance. Part of our family was missing. I'd say to the class, 'Does this person need support and how can we support her?' Or, to the social committee, 'Should we get a card?' This caring and support for each other every morning helped build our community of learners."

Teachers talked about being available before school and after, conducting home visits, and making intentional daily contacts—even if brief—with every student. Teachers also talked about continuing those relationships long after the student had left their classrooms. One example is María Antonia Piñón, who still keeps in touch with a cohort of her students through a Facebook group. She's still mentoring and providing support, long after retirement.

> ***From teacher to teacher***—*nothing is more important than the human connection. Make those connections every day.*

Value Teamwork

Making personal connections with families is often done individually. Providing program services to families most often takes a team. *Teamwork* doesn't come easily and is not a given when working in programs, but we do know that families benefit most when a team can come together to provide services for families in a big way.

Traditional family literacy programs have always operated within a team concept. Typically, early childhood or elementary teachers would team up with adult education or adult literacy teachers. Program administrators or coordinators were an integral part of the team. Some programs may have parent educators or home visitors. What we know historically is that teamwork and team planning are essential to the high-level functioning of programs.

One of the basic elements of teamwork in family learning programs is to set aside time for planning together. "We have devoted time for planning and discussing. We all have to be in this together, to best serve the family and be on the same page," said Katy Kibbey.

Some of the teachers interviewed spoke so strongly about the importance of team, that they were even reluctant to share and talk about their individual successes, and found it difficult to embrace the idea of receiving the award. Kay Brown said, "I get nowhere without the team around me. This is not a one-person show." Her supervisor shared in her nomination application that Kay "refuses to stand alone in the limelight for the program's accomplishments, stating repeatedly that successes are the result of the larger effort of the team."

Similarly, when Karen Klima-Thomas of Mesa, Arizona, was asked about receiving her award, she said, "When I accepted the award at the convention, I stated that I would not be up there were it not for Marilyn Box and the whole Family Tree team. I believe that to this day. Linda Mead [adult education teacher] and I clicked from the very first time we met. She was the best teacher partner I could have ever had." Cecilia Ramirez echoed that sentiment. "We all worked as a whole. A comprehensive team. We learned that by working together, the benefit is so powerful for parents and the children."

"My team was everything," added Karen Klima-Thomas. "My own team at my school and the Family Tree Program in total. We were so lucky to come together. I was so lucky to be a part of something that changed so many lives."

Additional elements of team building mentioned by the teachers included open communication, practicing teamwork daily, mentoring each other, helping each other out when needed, being flexible, and being willing to change plans. In addition, always remembering it's a team effort. No one flies solo.

From teacher to teacher—*it's not a one person show. It takes a village.*

Be a Learner

Throughout the interviews, the award teachers shared several personal habits important to each of them—things they did either every day, or habitually, that they felt contributed to their daily and/or overall success as a teacher. They practiced a variety of before school and after school routines, while also continuing their personal focuses of learning and reading every day.

"It's what you learn after you know it all, that counts." That quote has been attributed to many people, including winning UCLA Basketball Coach John Wooden. Professional baseball player Earl Weaver, wrote a book with that title. And Harry S. Truman, the 33rd President of the United States, supposedly said it too. Whoever coined the phrase, however, is not the focus here; it's the message—teachers never stop learning.

Like most educators, the majority of the award teachers continued their educational training and gained advanced degrees while maintaining their work with families. Continuing to *Be a Learner* is a mantra of our teachers. Many spoke of additional professional development offerings—trainings and certifications—that have supported them in their work with families. One teacher, Cecilia Ramirez, completed the trainer process to be a national certified trainer for NCFL, and all have attended the national NCFL conference/summit. Cecilia humbly says "I am also a learner." She believes in ongoing education and professional development. "The things I learned in professional development, I took back to my family literacy team and also to the parents."

When asked what advice she would like to share with other teachers, María Antonia Piñón quickly put 'being a learner' at the top of her list. She said, "First of all, be yourself. See yourself not as a teacher, but as a learner. If we remain in the mindset of being a learner, we walk in their shoes. Be a learner and grow from your own experiences, and from your students."

Along those same lines, Kristen Whitaker of Washington, DC, also said it was important to put herself in the shoes of her students and families, because then she's learning more about them. She also shared that it was important for her to keep up with international news each day. "How can I understand what troubles the immigrant families I serve, if I do not know what is going on in their countries and with their families?" Learning more about her families' cultures helps her to better understand her students, and build stronger relationships with them.

Mark Faloni summed it all up with this statement: "I get to teach my students English and the American culture, and they get to teach me life."

> *From teacher to teacher*—*learn in order to teach. Learn from your experiences and from your students.*

Be a Reader

It has often been said that we *learn to read*, so we can *read to learn*. There is no doubt that learning and reading go hand-in-hand, so it is no surprise that teachers excitedly shared their passion for reading. An important habit for them personally, they valued sharing that love of reading with children on the path to *Becoming a Reader*—but felt it was also important for teachers to continue to be readers, too.

Building on the love of learning and professional development, Katy Kibbey shared that it is important to her to continue to evolve as a professional and leader. "I read and stay abreast of the field and am always on the look-out for new approaches, ways to adapt and to ultimately do better. I recognize that while my roles and responsibilities have taken me out of the front lines, I still have a unique opportunity to add value to the mission of family literacy in particular and human services in general."

Family literacy programs have traditionally capitalized on that indispensable power of intergenerational literacy—of children and their parents enjoying books and literacy-based activities together. Reading, and passing along that love of books, is not only a central element of many of our teachers' programs, but a non-negotiable, essential element.

"I love, love, love to read," shared Dayle Bailey of North Carolina, "and I tried to pass along this love of reading to my family, my friends, and the families I worked with. I love it when reading becomes a fun, interactive, intergenerational event."

Jody Lintzenich of Nashville, Tennessee, believes that teaching children to read is a way of paying it forward. "Once children can read, they can do anything," she said. "For example, a little first grader I worked with in class and literacy just graduated from college last year with a degree in special education. She will in turn be teaching children. Inspiring children to be all that they can be is 'paying it forward' because they, in turn, will do that for someone else."

After adopting a Chinese infant, Jean Ciborowski Fahey, found herself thrust into the world of single parenthood. The experience inspired her to write the book, *Make Time for Reading*, a story guide for parents of young children. Jean shares that, "being an adopting parent provided a special connection between me and the families I work with. We share a common bond—each wanting the best for our children…" Jean's passion for reading, and helping young parents prepare their children for reading, is a common thread throughout her life and work.

Karen Klima-Thomas told us that giving books to children and to parents with new babies is one of her life's delights. "I read, read, read. I have always read, read, read. There is nothing that will serve a child better than growing a joy of reading."

As well, one of Kay Brown's greatest pleasures is introducing and sharing books to children and their parents. She has facilitated the distribution of thousands of books to at-risk children in her home community of Union Parish, Louisiana, and to children in the New Orleans area post-Katrina. Giving out brand new books to children at Christmas time is when Kay saw "children's desperation turn to joy." Known as the Louisiana Book Fairy, she and her colleagues have given out over two million books.

The love of books and reading can sometimes be difficult to nurture in cultures where an abundance of books cannot be found—particularly books in a child's native language or that represent his own culture. On the Gila River Reservation in Arizona, only a few elders speak the language and at least two generations do not speak the language at all. Books in the community are limited, and unfortunately, even fewer books exist in the native languages. Gwen Paul, early childhood teacher at Blackwater Community School, is a fluent speaker and uses every opportunity to teach culture to the children in her preschool classroom. She has worked with experts in the field of language and culture to create quality O'Otham children's books based on the history of the tribe, the Gila River, and the O'Otham people.

The power of reading—the power and pleasure of children and parents reading together—cannot be denied and is well-documented in research. This has also long been a message of NCFL. The warm feelings a child gets from sitting on a parent's lap and listening to a story, or exploring a book, go a long way toward growing a reader. When teachers value sharing books and the love of reading with children and their parents, parents begin to understand that kind of powerful experience for themselves.

From teacher to teacher—read, and share the love of books and reading with others.

Begin and End the Day

An educator's life is often defined by beginnings and ends. From the first day of school to the last, first drafts to final exams, and from the morning to the end-of-day bell—these beginnings and ends often are grounded in well-established habits.

We were curious about the teachers' daily habits—anything they did on a routine basis they felt contributed to their success as a teacher. Most of these habits manifested themselves into daily routines and fell into two categories—things teachers did at the *Beginning of the Day*, and things they did at the *End of the Day*, and we've listed them here as they said them. Most of these are personal to each teacher—yet, they may provide guidance or wisdom to others. Here are habits of these celebrated and highly effective teachers.

At the ***Beginning of Every Day:***
- I am available for my students before school.
- I make a one-on-one connection with every student, every day.
- I always take a full cup of empathy with me when I go to work each day.
- I begin every day with a grateful heart.
- I say a prayer.
- I pray every day.
- I arrive at school early.
- I am prepared.
- I am informed and prepared, so I can give my students my best.
- I am a creature of habit. A daily routine helps me prepare for learning.
- I check my first impressions of parents at the door.

From teacher to teacher*—be prepared in all ways. Students deserve your best, every day.*

At the ***End of Every Day:***
- I am available for my students after school.
- I reflect daily.
- I sit back in a chair and reflect on the day.
- I talk with my para-professional and we discuss the day—how it went, what we would do differently, what needs to happen tomorrow.
- I reflect and self-evaluate daily.
- I write in my journal every time students write in their journals.
- I input data daily.
- I re-evaluate and make adjustments.
- I ask:
    o What have I learned?
    o What am I grateful for?
    o What did I do today for someone else?

From teacher to teacher*—reflect. What will you do differently tomorrow?*

From Teacher to Teacher Summary

FOCUS ON FAMILIES
Put families in the forefront of everything you do.

PASSION AND ENERGY
Be passionate, enthusiastic, and positive. Love what you do, get out of your comfort zone, and enjoy the experience.

BUILD TRUST
Make sure students know they are valued, and that their contributions are welcome. Building trust grows out of knowing that teachers are sincere.

BUILD COMMUNITY
We all benefit from a community of support. We are stronger together than separate.

MAKE PERSONAL CONNECTIONS AND DEVELOP RELATIONSHIPS
Nothing is more important than the human connection. Make that connection every day.

TEAMWORK
It's not a one person show. It takes a village.

BE A LEARNER
Learn in order to teach. Learn from your experiences and from your students.

BE A READER
Read, and share the love of books and reading with others.

BEGINNING OF EVERY DAY
Be prepared. Students deserve your best every day.

END OF EVERY DAY
Reflect. What will you do differently tomorrow?

EVOLUTION OF FAMILY ENGAGEMENT

From the traditional era of the four-component, comprehensive family literacy model, to a focus on community involvement and service learning, to the digital learning communities of *Wonderopolis*® and *Family Trails*, the National Center for Families Learning (NCFL) has long been in the business of supporting family engagement and helping families learn together.

From Parent Involvement to Parent Engagement

In the past, typical parent involvement activities ranged from room mothers to school volunteers. Finding a single definition for parent involvement was not an easy task. The National PTA defined parent involvement "as the participation of parents in every facet of children's education and development from birth to adulthood, recognizing that parents are the primary influence in children's lives." Through the Elementary and Secondary Education Act, and many Title programs, school districts adhere to the federal legislation definitions of what parent involvement should look like, and what qualifies as parent involvement, in a public school.

NCFL considers parent involvement at a much deeper level. The heart of NCFL's work lies in its dedication to working with community partners to develop model programs that advance family literacy and encourage two-generation learning. NCFL has long recognized the need to move away from the terminology of "parent involvement" to terminology that better represents the rich, varied, and meaningful ways that parents interact with their children—all day, any day, and in a variety of settings.

The terms "family learning" and "family engagement" or "parent engagement" better represent the evolved NCFL vision. Our definition of parent or family engagement is all inclusive—from engaging and supporting parents in the educational processes of their children to positively impact their academic achievement, to supporting engagement as families learn, grow, serve, and find adventure together.

Traditional Family Literacy Models

Beginning with the Kenan Model and building from the federal definition of family literacy, NCFL's history is grounded in comprehensive family literacy services for families most in need. Parent-child interactions are the heart of these services and programs. Whether at home, in the classroom, or in the community, meaningful interactions lead to stronger parent-child relationships and cognitive growth for children. With the conception of Parent and Child Together (PACT) Time® in the late 1980s, NCFL defined parent involvement within a school program setting.

The federal definition of family literacy services brought continuity to traditional family literacy programs and is written into various pieces of federal legislation. NCFL implemented and supported many comprehensive family literacy programs based on this definition, including Even Start, the Family and Child Education (FACE) program, and the earlier Toyota funded school-based programs. The definition specifically reads:

"The term family literacy services means services that are of sufficient intensity in terms of hours, and of sufficient duration, to make sustainable changes in a family, and that integrate all of the following activities:

- Interactive literacy activities between parents and their children
- Training for parents regarding how to be the primary teacher for their children and full partners in the education of their children
- Parent literacy training that leads to economic self-sufficiency
- An age-appropriate education to prepare children for success in school and life experiences."

The first bullet, *interactive literacy activities between parents and their children* is the phrase that represents the meaningful parent-child interactions, or the Parent and Child Together (PACT) Time® component, of comprehensive programs. In a comprehensive program as described above, parents and children come to school together, to learn together. Children attend their own preschool classroom, while parents attend adult education/adult literacy classes. PACT Time, that interactive time between parents and children, happened for approximately one hour each day in the child's classroom. This structured time period was designed to support parents in the following ways:

- Assist parents in their role as first teacher of their children
- Help parents gain awareness of how children learn
- Provide parents with tools and strategies to support their children's learning
- Provide parents with an opportunity to practice interacting with their children in a supportive environment
- Support parents and help them feel comfortable with new ideas for parent-child interaction at school, home, or in the community

PACT Time—still a valuable and essential part of a comprehensive program for families most in need—has grown beyond the one hour of daily interaction in the classroom, to planned, frequent, and perhaps even random, teachable moments of exploration, adventure, and learning. The original goals of PACT Time were to improve speaking, listening, reading, and writing skills of parents and children, and to guide parents in understanding the value of positive interactions through play.

Not all programs can offer the level of intensity that comprehensive, four-component programs like Even Start, FACE, or Toyota-funded programs have offered—nor do many parents need or desire that kind of program intensity. Over time, as funding and program policies changed and evolved, NCFL sought ways to support meaningful parent-child interactions, or PACT Time experiences, that reached beyond the classroom and into the home and community.

The NCFL-Toyota Partnership

Toyota, one of the nation's most successful corporations, began a partnership with NCFL in 1991. With the generous funding from Toyota, NCFL has been able to grow family literacy and family learning programs across the nation. Major programs developed through the NCFL-Toyota partnership have influenced federal and state legislation and leveraged millions of dollars in additional funding to replicate, sustain, and grow family literacy programming.

The Toyota Families for Learning program was created in 1991 as an innovative approach to improving the education of preschool children and increasing economic stability within our country's most disadvantaged communities. This four-component program was inclusive of PACT Time, to support meaningful parent-child interaction. A total of 20 communities participated in this national program.

Established in 1998, Toyota Families in Schools was designed to increase achievement of at-risk children from ages 5-12 by implementing strong family literacy services in elementary schools. The program, which was implemented in 15 communities, emphasized parents' roles as learners, as well as supporters of their children's education. This initiative specifically targeted parents and their school-aged children who were deemed at risk of academic failure. PACT Time in the elementary school embraced the same basic goals as the preschool programs.

In 2003, the Toyota Family Literacy Program expanded to address the growing educational needs of Hispanic and other immigrant families in 30 communities by increasing English language and literacy skills for adults, while also supporting parents' involvement with their children's education. Communities engaged in this initiative have expanded and sustained services, adding more than $105 million to Toyota's initial investment in the process.

Community Involvement and Service Learning

Most recently, the NCFL-Toyota partnership has forged a new movement of families learning together, gaining new skills, contributing to their communities, and sharing what they've learned with other families—within and beyond school walls, on the go, and using technology.

Fueled by a family's imagination, the *Family Time Machine*™ turns a family's moments of togetherness into family time by learning, imagining, and playing. The *Family Time Machine* helps make the most of those moments by inspiring everyone to learn together with fun activities. Learn more about the *Family Time Machine* at familytimemachine.com.

The current NCFL-Toyota initiative is *Toyota Family Learning*, and it is built on the four cornerstones of Parent Time, PACT Time, Family Service Learning, and Family Mentoring. Fifteen communities have received funding to implement online and offline two-generation learning programs for vulnerable families. Each grantee hosts at least three major Family Service Learning projects per year. When children and families solve community issues together, they simultaneously learn and apply 21st century college and career readiness skills. To date (2016) participating families have spent more than 28,000 hours learning and serving together.

Digital and Mobile Engagement

Although the methods and strategies of supporting parent and family engagement can vary from structured, classroom-based programs to digital-based adventures—as long as parents and children come together, family engagement and learning can happen. Anywhere. Any time.

WONDEROPOLIS

Wanting to provide parents with an online resource that could be used at home to facilitate learning and drive dinnertime conversations, NCFL set out to create Wonderopolis, an online learning community that would help families foster and explore curiosities of the world. In 2010, Wonderopolis' debut Wonder of the Day® was, "Why are flamingos pink?" With the financial support of many partners, including Toyota, Wonderopolis.org now has more than 1600 archived Wonders, each of which feature corresponding videos, at-home activities, vocabulary quizzes, and more. NCFL's unique inquiry-based approach to learning was quickly adopted by educators for classroom and program instruction use in schools, libraries, and community-based organizations, leading to the Wonder Ground™—a Wonderopolis destination designed for educators—in 2016. Today more than 12 million children, parents, and teachers visit Wonderopolis.org each year.

Building on the success of Wonderopolis, NCFL sought to create a free out-of-school resource for families to help combat the well-researched and documented effects of summer-learning loss. Building upon the Wonderopolis model, NCFL launched what is now known as Camp Wonderopolis™ in 2012. Each year's virtual Camp features a newly themed online learning portal of 42 interactive Wonders full of fun STEM and literacy-building content and activities. In the last two years, these Wonderopolis "Campers" have earned more than 33,000 Wonder Cards™—collectible badges of achievement—by passing informational text quizzes and mastering 80,000 vocabulary terms. All Camps created since 2014 are available year-round on Wonderopolis.org and are used by educators looking to extend STEM- and literacy lessons.

TOYOTA FAMILY TRAILS

NCFL believes the family is the best teacher your child will ever have. That's why, in partnership with Toyota, we created Family Trails, an online community that builds upon NCFL's PACT Time to celebrate and inspire family adventures and anytime, anywhere learning.

Family Trails invites families to contribute stories and beautiful pictures of learning adventures ranging from trips to the park down the road to national parks and faraway lands. These stories help inspire families to think differently about their own lives and adventures, and to purposely seek out the learning moments in everyday life.

Driven by its social media community, *#FamilyTrails* has been adopted by families in all 50 states and 79 countries, achieving a potential reach of more than 7.7 million through Instagram and Twitter since its debut in June 2015.

You can download the newest edition of Trails Mix, a free magazine featuring the most inspiring learning adventures, recipes, activities, and stories from the Family Trails community at familytrails.com.

To find out more about other NCFL online learning communities, visit http://www.familieslearning.org/communities.htm.

Section Two

THE TOYOTA FAMILY LITERACY TEACHER OF THE YEAR AWARD

Historical Perspective

The *Toyota Family Literacy Teacher of the Year* award was established in 1997, with twenty outstanding teachers receiving this prestigious award through 2016. Those teachers are:

    1997 – Karen Klima-Thomas, Mesa, Arizona
    1998 – Anita Koch, Belle Glade, Florida
    1999 – Dayle Bailey, Rockingham, North Carolina
    2000 – Sharonrose McMarr-Schroeder, Los Angeles, California
    2001 – Cecilia Ramirez, Tucson, Arizona
    2002 – Gwendolyn Paul, Coolidge, Arizona
    2003 – Jody Lintzenich, Nashville, Tennessee
    2004 – Lorie Preheim, Washington, DC
    2005 – Amy Hall, Wilson, Michigan
    2006 – Mark Faloni, Washington, DC
    2007 – Gretchen Conway, Lenoir, North Carolina
    2008 – Katy Kibbey, Hamtramck, Michigan
    2009 – María Antonia Piñón, Miami, Florida
    2010 – Karen Kay Brown, Bernice, Louisiana
    2011 – Patricia Urdialez, Mesa, Arizona
    2012 – Shari Brown, Caldwell County, North Carolina
    2013 – Carolyn Blocker, Long Beach, California
    2014 – Elizabeth Atack, Nashville, Tennessee
    2015 – Kristen Whitaker, Washington, DC
    2016 – Jean Ciborowski Fahey, Weymouth, Massachusetts

The process for selection has been very effective over the years, with continuous improvements made each year in the implementation of that process. Over the years the award amount increased from $5,000 to $10,000, and to $20,000 in 2012. Several of the Teacher Profiles that come later in this book (Section 3) share how the programs utilized their award money to support their parent engagement programs.

The original title of the award was *Toyota Family Literacy Teacher of the Year* until 2012, when it was changed to *Toyota Family Teacher of the Year*. The new title gave opportunity to expand the award to teachers who do outstanding educational work with parents and children outside of the formal definition of family literacy programming.

Until 2012, there were typically two to three runners-up each year who each received a $500 award for the programs where they worked. In 2012, this award was increased to $2,500, and one runner-up was named, therefore making this award more prestigious. As of 2015, the runner up award was $5000. The winner and the runners-up received all-expense-paid trips to the National Center for Families Learning's (NCFL) National Conference on Family Literacy (now called the Families Learning Summit) where they were recognized for their accomplishments.

Often, additional support was provided for a family member's travel to conference. The winner and runners-up were recognized each year by a Toyota executive who announced the selections and presented the winner with a crystal apple at the Summit's all-attendee luncheon or banquet, and at a featured session of NCFL's conference/summit. Each winner spoke at a featured session of the conference, and the winner and runner-up participated in concurrent sessions where they discussed their program successes.

Changes in technology over the 20 years of the award contributed to modifications in the selection process. NCFL moved from requiring the applicants to submit hard copies of a type-written application, to using an online submission process. This has helped both NCFL and the nominator expedite the entire process. Applications are now submitted through the NCFL website, www.familieslearning.org.

Initially, the majority of the programs submitting nominations consisted of comprehensive family literacy programs. As funding streams changed and modifications to family literacy evolved, the types of programs submitting nominations changed. Today, community agencies, libraries, and teachers outside of the adult education and early childhood arenas are nominated.

Of the 20 awards, 17 were given to teachers who came from comprehensive family literacy programs.

Eight of the award teachers came from family literacy programs funded by Toyota. Starting in 1991 and continuing to the present (2016), Toyota has funded 280 program sites in 56 cities and 31 states based on the family literacy model of parents and children learning together.

Two award teachers came from comprehensive family literacy programs located on American Indian reservations and funded by the Bureau of Indian Education (BIE). Designed as an integrated model for early childhood and parent involvement for American Indian families, the Family and Child Education (FACE) programs have succeeded in addressing achievement gaps for American Indian children. The FACE program maintained the four-component, comprehensive model for approximately 25 years, until 2015 BIE regulation changes made allowances for children to enroll with relaxed participation from parents. Initiated in 1990, the FACE program currently operates in 46 BIE funded schools (2016-17).

In recent years, the award has branched out beyond the preschool/elementary school models to award one high school history teacher, one library program manager, and a hospital parent/teacher educator with the *Toyota Family Teacher of the Year award*.

Over the past 20 years, the award has been presented to

- 5 early childhood/preschool teachers, with one of those teachers also listed as the program coordinator.
- 11 adult education teachers, with 5 of those teachers focusing on English as a Second Language (ESL) instruction, and 3 of the adult education teachers also serving as the program coordinator.
- 1 elementary school teacher.
- 1 high school history teacher.

- 1 library program manager.
- 1 hospital parent/teacher educator.

Twelve of the award recipients currently work in the same program as they were when they received the award—most in their same position—and some may have added additional responsibilities such as program coordination. Two teachers have been teaching in the same classroom for the past 25+ years. Five of the award recipients have retired, with several of those teachers doing relevant volunteer work in the schools or in their community. Two teachers have moved on to other positions within their schools, and one teacher transferred jobs to another school district.

All of the programs shared that partnerships were important to their success. Programs provided various examples of collaborations throughout the years. Some of the most common partnerships were with: Head Start and Early Head Start, Smart Start, AmeriCorps, Social Services, community colleges, community libraries, Women-Infant-Child (WIC) programs, public schools, American Indian tribes, ESL programs, Community Action, state departments of education, health departments and behavioral health centers, museums, home visiting programs, and child care centers.

INTRODUCTION TO TEACHER PROFILES

Section 1 provided the highlights of effective practices shared by all of the Toyota teachers of the year and the evolution of family literacy and family engagement.

Section 2 provides an overview of the award and profiles for each *Toyota Family Teacher of the Year*, listed by the most current year to the past—2016 to 1997. Each profile shares information about the teacher and his or her program at the time of the award and current information about the teacher today.

The profiles include

- Quotes from parents or colleagues.
- Highlighted quotes from the teacher.
- Teacher responses to interview questions.

In addition, each teacher has provided three habits to share with other teachers. You will see these habits highlighted in a pull-out text box at the beginning of each profile.

Most of the 20 teachers provided responses to survey questions, while several teachers preferred phone interviews. Five teachers attended a focus group, and some questions interjected in this meeting have been included in their profiles. Sometimes teachers opted not to respond to a question, therefore not all questions occur in all profiles. Generally, NCFL was interested in learning more about the following:

- Do you have lessons learned you can share from your work in family literacy/family learning programs?
- If you could do anything differently today, what would you do?
- What is your motivation to keep working with families?
- How do you pay it forward?
- Do you have specific habits—things you do every day—that have helped you along the way?

Each profile is unique to each individual teacher and is written largely in her or his own words. The teachers were eager to share their practices, strategies, and habits that worked for them and hope they are beneficial for others.

NCFL hopes their stories and their expertise will provide guidance and inspiration to many practitioners in the field of family learning.

JEAN CIBOROWSKI FAHEY

South Shore Hospital Reading Partnership
Weymouth, Massachusetts

2016 Award Recipient

"[Jean] has been an unwavering stand for building parent capacities as a way to improve child outcomes. And given that the roots of literacy form in infancy, what better place than the birthing place to begin the conversations about preparing our children to be proficient readers?"

— Faye Weir, Director, Parent Child Services, South Shore Hospital

My Habits to Share

- Mistakes are okay. They are instructional.
- I honor my word.
- I check my first impressions of parents at the door.

Adopting a Chinese infant who had been abandoned at birth thrust Jean Ciborowski Fahey into the world of single parents. The experience inspired her to write the book, *Make Time for Reading*, a story guide for parents of young children, touted as an innovative, two-generation reading strategy. For Jean, being an adoptive parent provided a special connection between her and the families she worked with. They shared a common bond—each wanting the best for their children in the face of difficult circumstances.

> *I find parents to be great motivators because they are a source of ideas and wisdom.*

Jean Ciborowski Fahey, Ph.D., has been active in the field of early literacy for nearly 40 years. According to Faye Weir, Director of Child Parent Services at South Shore Hospital, Jean designed the South Shore Hospital Reading Partnership to "educate the community about the profound opportunity parents have to build a reading brain in a child's first five years, and thereby prevent many children from experiencing early reading problems." Jean teaches, blogs, and speaks on a variety of early literacy topics, targeting both parents and those who work with parents. Prior to working at South Shore Hospital, Jean assessed young children for reading difficulties at Children's Hospital/Harvard Medical School, worked as an adjunct language and literacy professor at Lesley University, and as an early literacy specialist with the national office of Reach Out and Read. In addition, she held a contract with the Massachusetts State Department of Education, Office of Adult Basic Education, where she coordinated family literacy services for Massachusetts' most vulnerable families.

Over the years, Jean has partnered with a number of organizations to help bring her workshops and materials to parents in various settings. Those partnerships include the Massachusetts Family Literacy Consortium, Massachusetts Department of Mental Health, and Child Life of Greater New York, where she designed a *Reading to Babies in the NICU* program for 11 New York Hospitals.

> *We now have hard brain data that show when we increase parent engagement beginning with the birth of their child and provide effective early childhood programs, we can not only improve child outcomes, we can benefit our society and increase returns on investments.*

Jean's book, *Make Time for Reading*, combines the evidence base behind how children's brains are hard-wired for reading early on, with a collection of parent questions about reading and how to teach young children to read. This picture book can be read aloud to children and also is designed as a learning tool for educators and parents.

Filled with parent tips and talking points, the book shares a once-upon-a-time-story about how a little girl gets ready to read. Says Faye Weir, "The more parents read the story, the more they learn how to build a foundation for reading in their own children. The illustrations and photos of [diverse] families bring to life the incredible journey of getting ready to read. And because the guide is written as a picture book, the messages are easily accessible to parents who cannot read well or who are learning to read English."

Make Time for Reading has been distributed to parents with infants in the Neonatal Intensive Care Unit (NICU) at Women & Infants Hospital of Rhode Island. Mellissa O'Donnell, Supervisor in the Partnering with Parents & Neonatal Follow-up Clinic there, shares that reading was not a familiar thing for parents who wait for their babies to grow big enough to go home. "But once they understood that even the tiniest of babies are listening for the voices of their parents, the books were readily used. Parents who otherwise would not expose their babies to books, get to take the books home to learn from and enjoy."

Self-published by Jean, and printed with generous philanthropic support, *Make Time for Reading* has been distributed to all mothers who deliver babies at South Shore Hospital, to local Head Start parents, and to local Reach Out and Read practices that support low-income families. The Spanish version of *Make Time for Reading* was translated in 2016.

In Her Own Words

Jean, what is your greatest lesson learned working with families?

The greatest lesson I learned from families is to listen to them.

Many years ago I conducted a needs assessment at a program for families without homes. For many weeks, I interviewed mothers enrolled in the program with questions about their attitudes, knowledge, and goals. It was clear to me these mothers had been asked these questions many times before. One day a mother stopped me in my tracks. "Listen," she said, "why don't you all ever ask us what we can do to help the program? Why is it that you are the only ones who get to help?"

I never forgot her questions and the huge lesson I learned that day. From this parent, I saw that I could learn as much from her as she could learn from me. That expanded my view of her as a mother and shifted my view of myself as both a professional and a mother.

From then on, when I interviewed parents, I would always end by asking, "Is there a question I did not ask you, that I should have?"

Looking back over your career working with families, if given the chance, would you do anything differently moving forward?

I regret that I never learned a second language. I say this because I know the inextricable link between language and culture. Speaking another language would have given me more insight into the world of many of the parents I work with—and a deeper appreciation of the challenge they face in learning English as a second language. This is one reason I had my book, *Make Time for Reading*, translated into Spanish.

What is your motivation to work with families?

What motivates me is finding innovative ways to translate the fascinating science of early child development in ways that excite and inspire all parents—especially those learning to read and speak English. I believe parents want to understand not just how to help their child get ready to read, but also *why* a family literacy practice makes a difference. This means I get to design simulations and demonstrations, and share stories that illustrate how parents and children can learn together. I also find parents to be great motivators because they are a source of ideas and wisdom.

The science also motivates me. That is, the increasingly accessible brain research that shows us how to build more promising futures for our most vulnerable young children and families. More specifically, we now have hard brain data that show when we increase parent engagement beginning with the birth of their child and provide effective early childhood programs, we can not only improve child outcomes, we can benefit our society and increase returns on investments.

Finally, I am motivated to work with parents because I am a parent. During my daughter's first years, I was a single parent. Adopting a Chinese infant who had been abandoned at birth, I was inspired by her to write *Make Time for Reading*. Being an adopting parent provides a special connection between me and the families I work with. Wanting the best for our children in the face of difficult circumstances is what we have in common.

Do you "pay it forward" to families or others who work with families? How?

In 2000, the South Shore Hospital CEO, Richard Aubut, championed my work by giving me a platform to teach a wide and diverse audience of early educators and expectant and new parents. To date, South Shore Hospital is unique as a hospital in its dedication to raising a generation of readers by institutionalizing the South Shore Hospital Reading Partnership. The Partnership not only serves families, but also engages the surrounding early education and care programs, business and child-advocacy programs in the get-ready-to-read conversations.

The CEO's belief in me has led me to pass on that belief to others who work with families of young children, especially our local Head Start teachers, nurse-home visitors, and most recently Latino professionals who work with our most vulnerable immigrant parents of young children.

It has been a privilege to "pay it forward" by making it possible for organizations to have donated 12,000 copies of *Make Time for Reading* to date. Free copies of the book have been distributed at birthing centers, literacy and library events, parent workshops, and national and state conferences. Parents take the story guide home to read and reread to their children. Increasing numbers of teachers are featuring the book in their own parent workshops and literacy events.

So for me, this is one way of "paying it forward"—when one has been given a gift and passes it on, without taking credit.

What are three "habits" or things you do on a regular basis that contributed to your successful support of families?

I make mistakes. "Mistakes are okay…indeed, they are instructional." When I heard one of the great teachers in my life say this in class, permission was granted for me to do the same. When I blunder and fail, I admit it and eventually ask for support and coaching. And often I create something new and better.

I honor my word. I model this in my teaching. For example, I tell my students, parents, colleagues that I am committed to starting and ending on time. When I can't keep my word, I clean it up and work to do better next time.

I check my first impressions about parents at the door. This often means I listen more than I speak. Sometimes, I must look past my own emotions to communicate as straight and respectfully as possible. I acknowledge to some, I do not know their language—but I do want to know them.

> *"I believe parents want to understand not just how to help their child get ready to read, but also why a family-literacy practice makes a difference."*
>
> — *Jean Cibrowoski Fahey, Ph.D.*

——— 2016 ———

KRISTEN WHITAKER

Columbia Heights Educational Campus
Washington, DC

— 2015 Award Recipient —

"Ms. Whitaker has the unique ability to bring history alive and engage ALL of her students. Our son was able to relate events in history to our present-day life experiences as a result of Ms. Whitaker's unique way of presenting the information."

— *Parent, Columbia Heights Education Campus*

My Habits to Share

- Take a full cup of empathy with you to work each day.
- Keep up with international news daily—to understand the troubles of immigrant families' home countries.
- Begin every day with a grateful heart.

When thinking of family engagement programs, we typically think of programs and activities that happen in early childhood (preschool) or elementary school classrooms—programs that have strong connections with adult education or adult literacy classes. Or, as in the case with families of infant/toddler children, programs that focus on home visiting.

Kristen Whitaker's work with family engagement and home visiting, however, takes off in a different direction. Kristen is the only high school teacher to receive the Toyota Teacher of the Year award. As a full time history teacher, Kristen works to engage families of her students through home visits. According to her principal, Maria Tukeva, Kristen has developed family engagement skills that go well beyond the expectations and imagination of the school. Maria shares that, "Through perseverance and continual learning, Kristen devised countless ways of using what she learned about families and students during home visits, to differentiate her classroom teaching."

> *I always take a full cup of empathy with me when I go to work each day. It is important that we are able to put ourselves in the shoes of our families. To try and help them, we need to understand them without judgement.*

Kristen's partnership for family engagement is with the Flamboyan Foundation, an organization she still works with today to train teachers city-wide to conduct home visits. The Flamboyan Foundation, with areas of focus in Washington, DC, and Puerto Rico, works to develop the capacity of educators to partner effectively with families so that children succeed. Kristen's work with the foundation has not only enhanced her own skills, but brought benefits to the teaching staff in her high school, where she conducts workshops on professional development days to leverage learning through home visits.

> *I enjoy giving families space and opportunity to learn and create together, as well as to talk about their future goals and plans, how they can help each other, and how I can help them as well!*

At Columbia Heights Education Campus (CHEC) Kristen teaches Washington, DC History, US History, and World History. At the time of her award, 90% of the 1400 student body at CHEC were minority families; 68% Hispanic or Latino; 28% African or African American; and 4% Asian or Pacific Islander. As a full-time teacher, Kristen works to constantly engage low-income minority families in the educational work of the school.

Principal Maria Tukeva wrote the following about Kristen in her nomination application for Toyota Teacher of the Year. "Kristen Whitaker is a beacon of enthusiasm for family engagement, a model for all others who aspire to learn how to better connect families to education, and an inspiration for teachers who may be apprehensive about making the visceral connection between home and school through home visits. For three years, our school has been granted by the Flamboyan Foundation the opportunity to receive training for enhanced connectivity between teachers and families. Kristen immersed herself in the cause and emerged as the leader, who conducted more home visits by far than any other teacher and diligently taught all other teachers about the benefits of striving to connect home and classroom."

Kristen's relationship with families might best be described by one of the parents she has worked with. "As a parent of more than one teen-age male child, I have learned that with them, comes teenage angst and insecurity. Both are normal personality traits on the path to adulthood. I've also learned that teenagers are often very picky about which adults they allow into their lives—both inside and outside of the classroom. They can identify adults who they think are disingenuous and don't really care about them, and they gravitate to those adults who are positive, encouraging, and supportive role models. Ms. Whitaker was, and remains, as one of the most positive, caring, and encouraging adults in our son's life. She has the highest integrity and honesty, and she is genuine and is extremely passionate about teaching.

I can unequivocally say that Ms. Whitaker was a primary factor in motivating our son to stay on the path to success—to persevere and to make good choices for his future. She referred to him as her little brother—and he accepted her wise counsel as his big sister. Ms. Whitaker celebrated the joy of his high school graduation with us and today, we still consider her part of the family. Ms. Whitaker is still very interested in our son's success and checks in with him periodically to encourage him to work hard and to continue to invest in his post-secondary education now, and for a bright future."

In Her Own Words

Kristen, considering your work with families, what is your greatest lesson learned?

As a teacher, sometimes it is easy to assume that parents or families do not care about their child's education, or are not interested in learning together as a family. That is not the case! Often times, families have to work harder to get time together. With the increase of technology, personal phones and tablets, families don't always make the time to learn together, or even talk to each other on a day to day basis. I enjoy giving families space and opportunity to learn and create together, as well as to talk about their future goals and plans, how they can help each other, and how I can help them as well!

What is your greatest regret, or failure, and how did it help you see, or do, things differently?

I would say my greatest regret or failure was failing three out of my four classes my first year in college, causing me to be placed on academic probation, along with the loss of my scholarship. Although I went to summer school, double majored, pledged a sorority, and graduated on time, I was never able to get my cumulative grade point over a 3.0, after starting with a .8! This made me see the concept of "balance" in a different light.

I learned that being studious doesn't mean no fun at all. It just means I have to prioritize and make time for what's important. This has made me a better educator, because I know the temptations my high schoolers face when deciding whether to hang out with their friends, or complete their homework. I can share my story with them including all the consequences I faced (summer school, plenty of loans). I can also encourage them to never give up! I could have returned home after my first semester and said it was too hard, or I didn't have what it takes. Instead, I picked myself up, developed better study habits, and kept my eyes firmly set on my goals.

Working with families can be stressful and exhaustive—what motivates you day after day?

What a heavy question! Prior to answering the call to teach, I was a financial aid rep at Trinity University. Unfortunately, I was always having to defend the students of DCPS (District of Columbia Public Schools) to my colleagues. They were under the impression that students from DCPS were not smart, had no family support, and had no effective teachers.

As a proud product of DCPS and the child of a highly effective teacher in DCPS, I was offended and most importantly, motivated. I quit my job and applied to be a substitute in

DCPS just to get the feel of being a teacher. After a year, I applied to work full time and was hired to teach History! My first year of teaching was when we rolled out the home visit program at my school. We were trained on the techniques of talking to parents and families and learning how we can support them. I was honestly a bit overwhelmed. And I was not comfortable with the time commitment I would have to give in order to complete these visits. Reluctantly, I tried one and had an immediate breakthrough. My relationship with that child grew through the roof! He was more attentive in class and he knew I truly cared about him and his future. After completing many of these visits, it occurred to me that I enjoyed getting to know the families I teach, and that the collaboration between teacher and family always benefits the students, family, and community as a whole.

As for what drives me, I would have to say my own family. I was, and still am blessed enough to come from a family that supports me in all of my endeavors. Growing up, I did not call it "family engagement" I thought my family was just nosey and I assumed all families were the same. I feel strongly that all families should have the same level of support I had and more.

Do you pay it forward? How do you do that?

I don't know if I "pay it forward," but I do offer help to any teachers who would like assistance establishing relationships with their families. I also assist my students and families anyway that I can. I attend events with them, shop for prom dresses, help with FAFSA completion, and whatever it is they need that I can supply.

What three habits do you have, that you feel contribute to your successful work as an educator?

I always take a full cup of empathy with me when I go to work each day! It is important that we are able to put ourselves in the shoes of our families. To try and help them, we need to understand them without judgement.

I am sure to keep up with international news each day. How can I understand what troubles the immigrant families I serve face if I do not know what is going on in their countries and with their families?

Last, but not least, I begin every day with a grateful heart! I was blessed to have a great education and strong family support and I would like to share that same type of love and support with the students and families I work with.

> *"[Kristen] has become, for students, the most sought after teacher on our campus. In her classroom, her students are highly engaged, and well above average in their academic success."*
>
> *~ Maria Tukeva, Principal, Columbia Heights Educational Campus*

Elizabeth Atack

Nashville Public Library
Nashville, Tennessee

--- 2014 Award Recipient ---

"Whether we are talking to the parents of a newborn or the parents of a fourth grade student, our main message remains the same: If you make parent-child experiences with books and literacy positive and fun, they will be motivated to read."

— Liz Atack

My Habits to Share

- Remember that parents are the experts on their children.
- Be positive!
- Meet parents where they are.

Elizabeth (Liz) Atack works at the Nashville Public Library (NPL), where she oversees Bringing Books to Life (BBTL). In addition to managing the program's daily and long range operations, she is on the front lines of helping kids learn (and love!) to read, juggling story times, trainings for teachers, and reading workshops for parents. Under her leadership, BBTL has won local and national awards. Locally, Liz is the Vice Chair of Alignment Nashville's Pre-K Team and serves on advisory boards for local early education and parent engagement organizations. Before coming to NPL in 2007, Liz was a teacher and museum educator. She graduated from Oberlin College in Oberlin, Ohio, and possesses a master's degree in Childhood Museum Education from Bank Street College of Education in New York City.

Bringing Books to Life (BBTL) is a literacy outreach program of the Nashville Public Library, supported by the Nashville Public Library Foundation. BBTL offers programming to partner organizations that serve the educational needs of young children, adults, and families in the community. With a goal of fostering a love of books and library use, BBTL hosts family events at the libraries, and throughout the community. Under Liz's guidance, BBTL launched Loving & Learning family literacy workshops, the impact of which has been significant. At the time of her award, over 6,000 parents and families had participated in the workshops, with 100% reporting they learned more about literacy development, and 99% reporting they were more inclined to use the library after taking the workshop. BBTL serves any program serving young children and families, regardless of income level, including Nashville's large and growing immigrant and refugee community.

Today, in 2016, Liz is still in her same position at the Nashville Public Library. She shares, "We are still humming along, training teachers, providing parent workshops and doing outreach to preschools. The year before I received the award, we launched our adult literacy component. Like the rest of BBTL, we are focused with providing outside service providers access to library resources and opportunities to enhance what they are already doing in the classroom through professional development for teachers and programs/presentations for adult learners. Now, we are three years into our adult literacy programming and we have really become the hub for adult education/literacy in the city. That's exciting! I've been delighted by the cross-over impact of our adult literacy programming onto BBTL's other components, too. One of the services we offer is a mobile laptop lab that we can bring to an organization for lessons—given either by the organization or our staff. Many of the staff at the childcare centers we serve lack basic computer skills. We're able to give them basic lessons on how to use the computer, how to use the library's online resources and tie it into how they can use these skills in the classroom.

"Another update is that BBTL now has a full-time, fully-bilingual Family Literacy Coordinator. She came on board full-time last January, and the impact has been dizzyingly tangible! Our capacity to provide workshops has skyrocketed, and her bilingualism has allowed us to forge some key partnerships that help us reach Nashville's newest Americans. We have been working closely with the local public health department's Woman-Infant-Child program on two initiatives: first, to use library locations as Mobile WIC sites, bringing more families into the library and second, to provide literacy workshops as part of WIC's monthly workshop offerings. Since June 2015, we have been offering two workshops per month at one of the WIC clinics. One workshop is always in English and one is always in Spanish. These have been extremely successful—so much so that we are considering expanding to other WIC clinics. We've also forged a closer relationship with the newly-expanded Pre-K department at Metropolitan Nashville Public Schools, offering regular workshops districtwide, and with our local Head Starts, offering workshops at all of their locations."

In Her Own Words

How has winning the teacher of the year award influenced your family education practice?

I don't know that the award changed my practice, per se, but I think that winning, because I'm from a library, has helped us to gain some attention. Libraries have always felt that they are educational institutions, but whether or not the communities around them think that—usually they don't. Me having won the award really kind of helped solidify my library's place in the community as an educational institution. I think it's helped other libraries as well. That's actually been very personally meaningful to me, that we've helped round that corner.

How did your program utilize the funds that came to your program because of this award?

I've been using the funds to do some intentional outreach to our refugee and immigrant community in Nashville. This kind of programming doesn't really fall under our regular budget allocations. It's not part of our current logic model, so it didn't really have a place, but it was something that I felt very strongly that we needed to explore. The funds really let us make some intentional in-roads with that community. We've been doing targeted events for refugee and immigrant families through two different partners. The funds have let us purchase books, food, and really put on robust experiences for these families, that let them know that the library cares about them and is interested. And that the library's there for them.

What is your greatest lesson learned working with families?

It may seem like an obvious lesson, but every time I work with families, I am reminded that all families love their children and want the best for them.

What is your greatest regret/failure, and how did it make you do things differently?

I am struggling with this question! There are many times when, after a workshop or interaction with a parent or child, I wish I had responded differently. I think we all have had those moments. I do remember that we had some workshops early on where I realized the workshop I was presenting was not the workshop that was most appropriate for the audience present. For example, we had one workshop that we prepared to present as a parent-only workshop, but it ended up being parent and child. We also had a workshop—intended for parents of children ages three to five—where brand new parents and parents of elementary school students showed up! From those early experiences, I realized not only the importance of communicating expectations on the front end, but also how crucial it is to get to know the families in the room with you, and to be prepared to modify a workshop at a moment's notice. Unlike many programs, we do not see the same groups of families regularly—we may see a family once and never again, or, we may present a full series of workshops and see families as many as five times over the course of a school year.

Being able to switch directions once a workshop has already begun means that you have to know quite a lot about early literacy and know to whom to refer parents when you don't know the answer to their questions. It means that, for me and my staff, there is always more to learn and incorporate into workshops. And, it's good to remember that, whether we are talking to the parents of a newborn or the parents of a fourth grade student, our main message remains the same: If you make parent-child experiences with books and literacy positive and fun, they will be motivated to read.

What led you to this calling? What is your passion and why does it drive you?

In college, I majored in Anthropology and Archeological studies and thought I would go into academia. About halfway through my college experience, I realized that I didn't want to pursue a graduate degree in either subject, but I still liked learning about them and I wasn't sure what I was going to do. One day, I saw a sign in the library advertising the college art museum's student docent training program. I had an "a-ha!" moment and applied. I ended up working at the museum, giving tours and assisting with family and children's programming until I graduated. After college, I tried to find a job in museums, but they were few and far between (and highly competitive!), and so I ended up working as a kindergarten assistant teacher at a private school in Nashville. I loved it! After a little research, I found Bank Street College of Education in New York City. They offered a master's degree in museum education that led to teacher certification, which seemed like the best of both worlds for me.

One of the great things about Bank Street and the museum education program is the emphasis on children and their contexts—the family and community that surround them. In my student teaching placements, I worked with teachers who involved families and familial networks heavily in the classroom. One teacher regularly invited family members in to be interviewed by the class, and these interviews were fodder for classroom books, murals, and children's research. They also worked to foster community within the classroom—an interview with a family member of a child who was new or struggling in the classroom was a great way to draw that child into the community. It also created a classroom where all parents felt welcome and important.

After finishing up at Bank Street, I worked for about two-and-a-half years in a museum, first as the school programs manager and then as the education director, but felt like something was missing. Then, while doing some soul-searching, I happened upon an opening at Nashville Public Library managing a grant-funded early literacy program, Bringing Books to Life. It sounded like it would be a good way to utilize my skillset, and it sounded like it would be fun! It was also advertised as temporary, which I thought would give me some time to really figure out what I wanted to be when I grew up. I've now been here for a little over 9 years, so I guess I've figured that out! Shortly after I came on board, we started throwing around the idea of offering workshops for parents. We had done them before— here and there, as requested—but didn't have an actual program component for families. It made sense—BBTL had developed great relationships with child care providers and early childhood educators. But, the current model only had one point of contact with families. We felt like we could do better and got to work developing a workshop for parents, and one for parents and children together, on sharing and talking about books. I remember being nervous, because working with families felt so far outside of my area of expertise. Once we got going, though, I found that I loved working with families. Teaching them that they could read pictures instead of words, opened up so many doors for parents who had limited literacy skills or who spoke a language other than English. Showing parents the benefits of the things they were already doing with their children—singing, talking, playing—didn't just educate parents; it gave them a pat on the back and *empowered* them. And, we directed them to resources that are free and available to anyone. That's what really excites me and helps me maintain enthusiasm for a workshop where just one or two parents (out of an expected 20) show up. We are empowering parents as their child's first teachers.

BBTL has grown a lot, and I don't get to do parent workshops as frequently as I used to. More often, I get to "talk-up" all the great ways we could help families help their children love reading. I do get to help with workshops on occasion, though. Each time I am reminded of why I love them and why they are so important. By working with childcare centers and preschools to lead these workshops, we are also helping those agencies develop a more robust relationship with their parents and giving them parent-friendly language to use when they talk about literacy. That extends our reach well beyond our capacity to provide workshops—we are changing how preschools and teachers interact with parents! And, that takes me back to the classroom I worked in back in 2002, where my teacher-mentor made parents and community an integral part of her classroom, which strengthened the classroom community as a whole. When you involve the whole family, you get so much more than "family involvement!"

Do you pay it forward?

I don't know about paying it forward, but would like to share some wisdom that a mentor teacher shared with me when I was student teaching in her classroom. She impressed on me the importance of transcending whatever is happening in my personal life, and putting my focus on the students. Some days that's hard—I have bad days like everyone else—but I'm a big believer that everyone has their cross to bear and that mine is my responsibility and no one else's. I know the parents or teachers who are in my workshops are tired. They've worked a long day and they are choosing to spend time with me to learn something about reading with their child. My only responsibility is to give them a positive, enriching experience, so that's what I strive to do.

What are three habits or practices that you do consistently, that may have contributed to your successful support of the families?

Establishing that, while I'm an expert on education and literacy, I am not the expert on their child or their child's development. I try to share what I know and help parents apply that knowledge to their unique situation.

Positivity! Rather than telling parents about all the wrong things they're doing, I try to offer them tips and ideas about what they could do and explain why it's a good thing to do. Often, parents are already doing some of these things (talking with or singing to their child, for example), and giving them encouragement to trust their instincts and to go with what they know is very empowering for them.

Meeting them where they are. I'm not talking emotionally or psychologically, but physically. Our workshops have been so successful because we try to operate like water—we travel along the path of least resistance. We do workshops where parents already are—at their child's school or daycare, for example—and we do them at times that work for them. This means we do workshops as early as 8 am, or as late as 7 pm. It can make for long days, but it's worth it!

Carolyn Blocker

Long Beach Family Literacy Program,
Long Beach, California

—— *2013 Award Recipient* ——

"I had multiple attempts to get my diploma. My family had lost hope for me because I kept failing at it. Mrs. Blocker gave me the confidence I needed to set short and long-term goals. When I got my final test scores that said I was graduating, she was the first person I called. We both cried."

— *Julia C., Adult Education Student, Long Beach Family Literacy Program*

—— *My Habits to Share* ——

- Listen between the lines.
- Be willing to throw away the lesson plan.
- Empower everyone, including yourself!

Before Carolyn Blocker began teaching in the Family Literacy Program at Long Beach, she worked with struggling first grade readers in the Reading Recovery program, where she says she "shared in the joy of my students as they read text independently for the first time." This victory was shared by student and teacher—but Carolyn realized there was a very important missing component. The parent. Then along came Family Literacy.

> *With Family Literacy as a foundation, parents become more confident, children become more prepared, and families become more successful.*

Carolyn shared in her Teacher of the Year application, "It was during my first year in Family Literacy that I realized the parents I worked with needed that empowerment as well. I worked hard to show parents the world so they could introduce that world to their children by simply engaging with them. I wanted to embrace the idea that they are their children's first and most important teacher! I knew that would be my task. My parents needed confidence in themselves and confidence in their relationships and parenting skills." She added that, "I also get to be the happy observer who has the pleasure of watching parents love their children a little more each day. With Family Literacy as a foundation, parents become more confident, children become more prepared, and families become more successful."

In her position as parent educator in the Long Beach Family Literacy Program in Long Beach, California, Carolyn Blocker worked hard to eliminate that missing component by empowering parents as their children's first teacher and extending learning to the home.

Since 1992, the Long Beach Family Literacy program has focused on serving families with children ages one to five years, through the comprehensive, four-component program. These components include: Adult Education, Parent Education, Parent and Child Together (PACT) Time®, and Early Childhood Education. At the time of Carolyn's award in 2013, adult students took classes at the Long Beach School for Adults, while their children attended either the Program's Early Head Start toddler center, or Head Start preschool classes. Weekly, parents came together for parent education, where they learned parenting skills and gained support to be their child's best teacher. An interactive literacy component (PACT Time) allowed parents to come together with their children to play and learn side-by-side, putting their parenting skills into action. The families attending the program are 95% below the federal poverty level and 80% dual language learners with adults re-entering school to learn English, earn a high school diploma, or get a GED. The program serves language learners such as Japanese and Arabic.

> *The greatest lesson I have learned about families is, that we all need a community of support to be successful.*

Long Beach Program Coordinator, Roberta Lanterman, shares that, "In her first few years, Carolyn improved the lives of over 300 families. The program saw significant parent engagement outcomes as documented by our yearly outside evaluation. Results indicated the adults made significant progress with the respect to supporting their children's learning environment at home and their role in interactive literacy activities by making at least a full point gain in each subscale. This and other achievements, such as increases in retention and attendance, is a true testament to Carolyn's ability to reach our parents and keep them engaged in their own learning and working with their children."

> *I think our goal as educators should be to empower others, not just the students that we work with but our colleagues as well. We are stronger together.*

Today, Carolyn still works with adults learners, as an ESL instructor for the Long Beach Unified School District. She works with the parents of students attending Bobbie Smith Elementary School, and shares that, "Our ESL lessons are infused with ideas and strategies for navigating the school system, as well as building strong families."

Her favorite job, though, she says, "Is being the mom to three great kids, Thomas (20), William (17) and Anna (13). I am also fortunate to be the Children's Ministry Director at my church. This is my 28th year in education. After spending the last 10 years working with families, I am returning to the elementary classroom this fall. The skills I have learned while being a part of the Family Literacy program will benefit me as I take on this new, old experience."

In Her Own Words

What are some lessons learned you would like to share?

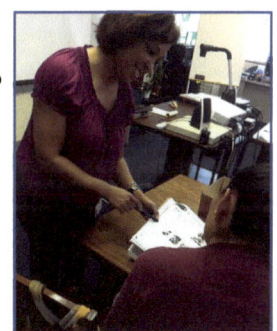

The greatest lesson I have learned about families is that we all need a community of support to be successful. We all have a shared goal of helping our children achieve their greatest potential. No matter what family you are a part of, this feeling transcends culture, race, religion and economic status.

From your experiences working with families, is there anything you would do differently?

If I had it to do over again, I would have realized the potential for this "ride" to end. I was fortunate to be part of a successful program that from year to year managed to get funded against all odds. I often made the mistake of thinking, "I can't wait to try that next year…" not realizing that "next year," might not come.

What motivates your work with families?

My first year of Family Literacy, I remember thinking I have the best job in the world because I get to encourage parents to love their children as much as I love mine! Even after all this time, I still get so excited watching people grow in their relationships. What I noticed is that by sharing experiences, it leads to confidence and that confidence creates a self-esteem that allows relationships to grow. Nope, I never get tired of being part of that journey and experiencing it myself.

How do you pay it forward?

The school where I currently teach received a significant community schools grant. They are partnered with the YMCA. While I no longer specifically teach parenting classes, I often share ideas for a successful Parent Center programming with the YMCA coordinators. It would be easy for me to just walk out at the end of my lesson about subject-verb agreement, but my heart calls me back to make sure the needs of the parents are being met. I think our goal as educators should be to empower others, not just the students that we work with but our colleagues as well. We are stronger together.

Do you have habits you feel have contributed to your teaching success?

Listen between the lines to what someone is really trying to tell you. The more you understand the situation, the more you can be helpful.

Be willing to throw away the lesson plan, what you planned is not necessarily what your group may need.

Be empowering to everyone, including yourself!

> *"Sharing experiences leads to confidence, and confidence creates a self-esteem that allows relationships to grow."*
>
> *— Carolyn Blocker*

Shari Brown

Caldwell County Family Literacy Program
Caldwell County, North Carolina

———— **2012 Award Recipient** ————

"Shari Brown is truly a dedicated and superb professional who is changing the world one student at a time through her outstanding instruction and program leadership."

— *Melinda Hefner, Family Literacy Colleague*

———— *My Habits to Share* ————

- Build relationships. Make a personal connection with every student.
- Set goals.
- Involve students in all aspects of program planning.

When asked what motivates her to work with families, day in and day out, Shari Brown provides this quote:

The most important tool for success is the belief that you can succeed.

"In high school," Shari shares, "I discovered that teaching is more than just the day-to-day interactions between curriculum and students. I had a teacher who always got to know her students personally. She made an effort to get to know each of her students' strengths and was able to use them to help her students excel in life. She encouraged me to believe I could succeed educationally as well as personally, and in the process, gave me the desire to become a great teacher like her. As a result, I make a conscious effort every day to enhance self-esteem and build confidence in my students and their families. Not a day goes by that I do not have numerous students in my office talking with me about their daily lives, both challenges and successes. My morning visits from families are my favorite part of each day.

"Over the years, I have discovered that in order to be a successful family literacy instructor it is important to provide my students with a comfortable, accepting learning environment that combines their educational and personal goals. Every day I interact with and listen intently to my students and learn from their individual perspectives and life experiences. Having that connection with my students allows me to use their interests and needs as a foundation for my lesson and teach in a holistic manner. Overall, I believe that if I treat my students with respect as equals in experience and knowledge and allow them to express themselves freely in class, my students are successful in achieving their short- and long-term goals. The ultimate reward is seeing my students succeed in life. When they come back to share both their successes and challenges with me, I realize that not only do they hold a special place in my heart, but I hold a special place in their lives also."

If you do not first make a personal connection with your students and allow time for a relationship, they will not trust you with their educational and personal pursuits.

In 2012, Shari Brown coordinated and worked as the adult education instructor at the Caldwell County Family Literacy Program. In operation since 1997, the Caldwell County Even Start Family Literacy Program was located in Western North Carolina, in a county ravaged by the results of the off shoring of the manufacturing industry. High unemployment rates and accompanying social issues left families with many struggles. The program offered two comprehensive, four-component family literacy sites. In partnership with Caldwell Community College, Caldwell County Schools, Early Head Start, Smart Start, and the Family Infant and PreSchool program, the family literacy program strived to reach families with children from ages birth to seven years. Adult students worked to obtain a GED, attend ESL classes, and learn more about parenting and supporting their young children's academic achievement.

Shari started the program and served as the Adult Educator/Coordinator for the life of the program. According to Program Director Pam Fultz, the program's "Ongoing success is due in large part to her skill as a teacher, mentor, counselor, trainer, and administrator." As a result of Shari's work, children enter kindergarten ready to learn, speak English well, and with parents who are active and productive participants in their children's education. Shari takes parents beyond the classroom doors to participate in activities that can affect their entire lives. The family literacy program has been a positive backdrop for success for many families.

Today, Shari is still involved with the program; however, their situation has dramatically changed. She shares, "When I received the Toyota National Family Literacy Teacher of the Year in 2012, I was the Adult Education Coordinator and Instructor of the Caldwell County Even Start Family Literacy Program. Almost immediately upon my return from receiving the award, our program was notified that federal Even Start funding was going to end. With the lack of Even Start funding, our program went from a budget of $336,000 a year (federal and state funding) to $86,000 a year (state funding only). Last year, state comprehensive family literacy funding ended, so now our local community college is funding the program. We have numerous collaborators in the community, but funding sources are scarce. As a result of the demise of Even Start funding, the program lost our director, early childhood coordinator, and four early childhood teachers. At this point, I became the director of the program with duties including overall coordination of the early childhood and adult education components, daily director duties, recruitment/retention, and grant writing, not to mention instruction in our ABE/GED/ESL classes on a daily basis. It has been very challenging to say the least, but I am determined not only to keep our program running, but also to provide high quality services for our families."

In Her Own Words

Shari, you've had many successes working with families. What is your greatest lesson learned?

I do not have one particular curriculum, nor do I teach solely through textbooks. I have learned that the best way to teach in a family literacy program is to observe personal interactions and elicit feedback from families and use that information to create curriculum and daily lessons. As an instructor, we should not teach the same curriculum year after year in the same order. For example, every February the lessons should not have to revolve around Valentine's Day, presidents, and mail. If families are interested in transportation and trains at that time, then that should be the focus of the month. Meeting with the family literacy team (director, early childhood teachers, adult educators, parent educators, and home visitors) once a month to discuss the interests and needs of the families is the best way to decide on the focus concept of the month for the program as a whole. Integration of the components and creating a shared vision is integral to the success of a family literacy program. In order to reach students of all ages, levels and backgrounds, the program tries to make learning interesting and relevant. Curriculum ideas always come from the individual students' interests and needs. This is done through many different strategies including but not limited to: Project based learning activities, novel based lessons, journaling, and contextualized learning opportunities.

What is your greatest failure, and how did it make you do things differently?

When working in family literacy, every day is an experience in problem solving. Families enter our program with issues that range from lack of housing or transportation to child rearing difficulties and domestic violence. A lack of education is what qualifies an individual to be part of our program, but this is not always the first issue that needs to be addressed when a family enrolls.

I am constantly reminded of Maslow's hierarchy of needs when working with this population. Until an individual's basic needs are met, other needs cannot even begin to be addressed. The process of dealing with these issues alone can be very difficult to navigate, not to mention adding barriers, such as language and cultural differences. Twenty years ago, I remember making phone calls myself to find community resources, going grocery shopping, and loaning money to my students. It did not take me long to realize that I was not helping anyone by "doing things" for my students. As the parable goes instead of "giving a student a fish," I have learned to "teach my students to fish." When my students come to me with very challenging issues, I have found that if I am flexible with my lesson plans and my class schedule, these challenges can become some of the best teaching/learning experiences put into practice.

How do you pay it forward?

A grant from GlaxoSmith Kline enabled the Director of Counseling and Advisement Services from Caldwell Community College and me to develop the Life Transitions through Literacy curriculum, also known as the Ribbon of Hope/Self Esteem curriculum. Use of the curriculum seeks to raise the literacy levels of students participating in ABE/GED/ESL programs through the use of an integrated reading and writing program that emphasizes building self-esteem, maintaining personal mental health, and developing internal coping strategies that lead to successful educational outcomes through increased persistence and more meaningful participation in the program. My philosophy is that if a student comes to class with immediate life-altering issues, all lessons are dropped, and the student's immediate needs are addressed. This curriculum focuses on students' personal well-being and addresses these issues proactively instead of having to address issues in a reactive way. Through this curriculum students see how education is integral to improving their lives overall rather than expecting them to choose between taking care of their lives or taking care of their education. I have had the opportunity to share this curriculum at local, state, and national conferences.

If you could name three habits—things you do on a regular or daily basis—that have helped to support your success working with families, what would they be?

> *"No significant learning occurs without a significant relationship."*
>
> — Dr. James Comer

I believe in the statement above by James Comer. I believe in seeing my students first as people on a journey, and then seeing them next as students enrolled in a program that happens to be part of that journey. My teaching role is larger than being just an instructor. From the first time I meet a student it is always about one human being beginning a relationship with another human being. I share personal challenges and life experiences with my students and in return they share with me. If you do not first make a personal connection with your students and allow time for a relationship, they will not trust you with their educational and personal pursuits.

When families begin class with me I sit down with them individually and we discuss short and long term goals. This process is recorded on a "Plan for Success" document. I facilitate the conversation that leads to the development of family goals, identifying possible barriers for reaching those goals, and brainstorming solutions and resources. The family and I revisit this plan on a monthly basis. I make sure that each family has focus and direction every day, following up with intentional and documented progress toward reaching their goals.

I always involve students in the planning and implementation of all components of the family literacy program. From interest assessments to family focus groups, students are active participants in all aspects of program development and curriculum. I want it to be their program, not mine.

> *"Thanks to the great encouragement and cooperation of Shari Brown, I graduated with my GED and today I am a student at the college. I still miss her and remember her as my excellent and wonderful teacher; someone who gave me a hand to another step of success in my life."*
>
> — Eliana Tamayo, Student, Caldwell County Family Literacy Program

Patricia Urdialez

Longfellow Elementary School
Mesa Public Schools Family Literacy Program
Mesa, Arizona

―――― **2011 Award Recipient** ――――

Pat [Urdialez] taught me that no matter what happens in my life, I can still be my best for myself and my family."

— *Araceli Cervantes, Mesa Family Literacy Program*

―――― *My Habits to Share* ――――

- Pray every day.
- Be prepared.
- Work to build community.

When others describe Pat Urdialez, the one word that often rolls to the surface is energy. From colleagues to students, and even when Pat shares information about herself, the word energy is not only a theme, but is also felt.

Christine Niven, Family Literacy Coordinator of Mesa Public Schools says of Pat, "When you walk into her classroom, you can feel the energy. She is usually running around helping students, laughing, and smiling. Her class is full of people and everyone is working. No one is ever bored because she is always well prepared and knows her students' goals and needs. She takes care to plan her lessons to address the individual needs of each of her students. Administrators and colleagues who observe her become so engaged with her teaching, they often tell me they have lost track of time. Her students ask her, 'Where do you get so much energy? Can you give me some?' It's difficult to capture Pat's many qualities on paper, and even more difficult to convey the enthusiasm, good humor, and kind-heartedness that are characteristic of Pat. She is admired and respected by the Longfellow school staff, her students, colleagues, and me."

> *When my students share their successes with me, it gives me more energy, and more passion, to do even more.*

A mother herself, Pat says she is on a quest to educate parents and help them to build special connections with their children. She subscribes to the "it takes a village" philosophy of raising a child and commits her dedication and determination to make a difference in her own students' lives. Christine Niven also adds that, "Pat has had obstacles in her life, and she has managed to raise three wonderful, successful children on her own. Now, being a single mother has given her an extra push to make a difference in our community."

To that, Pat adds, "I have always loved teaching… I have often been told that I take it too personally. I guess that is probably correct; it is personal to me. That is what makes family literacy a good fit for me. It comes naturally. I use a lot of the same strategies and ideas I did as a mother of my own children. My students are family and I take a very personal stand at how I teach them, and what I teach them. I hold them to the same standards that I hold my own children. In the end, I hope to have enriched my students' ability to think about, discuss and apply these skills in their lives, and with their family. It is so fulfilling to be a part of students' learning, responding to and applying what I have to offer. To see the change and improvement in the students' abilities, and in their family life. Family literacy makes my job as a teacher indescribable."

At the time of her award in 2011, Pat had been working at the Longfellow Literacy Program at Longfellow Elementary School for three years, with seven years prior experience in education. The Longfellow program is part of the Mesa Public School system in Mesa, Arizona. Originally funded by Toyota through NCFL, in 2011 the program was three years old. Christine Niven shares that "During the first year the program struggled. Then came Pat." Her energy and enthusiasm took hold and the program blossomed. Soon there was a waiting list of families, and after a couple of years, an evening program was added. Pat also teaches those classes. The success of the program has been recognized at the Mesa district level. Other principals were soon interested in having the program at their schools, and Title I began sustaining the programs after the Toyota funding ended.

Today, Pat is still at Longfellow teaching adult students, but she holds the additional title now of Career Pathways Coordinator.

In Her Own Words

In the classroom, my goal is to create an atmosphere that encourages participation and involvement. I invite my students into a relationship with family literacy, with me, and with each other—a community bonded with similar goals and experiences. Students are encouraged to come to my room at any time, to discuss ideas, plans, and concerns. I engage students with vibrant examples and stories, usually personal. This allows my students to feel comfortable and participate.

I believe in a flexible manner of instruction, responsive to the unique atmosphere of my class. I am sensitive to the students' backgrounds and goals, aiming to connect with their personal experiences. Students are at the center of my lesson planning process.

I take advantage of every opportunity to empower my students with specific strategies and ideas, so they will be able to converse and interact confidently in English, with whomever they encounter and ultimately, they will teach these strategies to their children.

After working in adult education for several years, I was lucky to have the opportunity to work in family literacy. Although I am still an adult educator, family literacy is so much more, and I feel like it is a natural fit for me. It gives me the opportunity to make a difference in families' lives that I never experienced before.

How has winning the teacher of the year award influenced your family education practice?

I stumbled upon being an educator. I was in the business world for many years, and I was miserable. When my youngest child was small, I went to Kindergarten along with him. I spent a lot of time volunteering, and then eventually was asked if I was interested in being a teacher assistant. I was. Eventually, I went back to school to get my degree and started teaching. I never knew I could be so passionate about my job, my career. My students are my motivation, my energy. The reason I come to school every day.

Receiving the award helped in that we all—the staff and the families—received recognition in the district. This recognition was for our program, and we felt we had earned overall respect.

I also felt more responsibility to do a good job. With this title came additional responsibility. I knew I was a good teacher, but I wanted to be an even better teacher. It was an eye-opener for me, that someone else would recognize that I am a good teacher. I remember saying to my coordinator, Christine Niven. "I'm just doing my job. Doesn't everybody do their job this way?" I only know how to give 100% in everything I do.

Getting the award was almost an uncomfortable thing to accept. I had to think about how I was going to act, because it was an uncommon place for me to be. I decided to accept it, embrace it, and use it however I could to make my class better.

What is your greatest lesson learned from working with families?

I think the greatest thing I have learned is how much the students appreciate me. That my effort, my time, is important to them.

I am a high-energy person. This is who I am and it works for me.

I believe in the impact that I have on them. If I show them energy and passion, it will come right back to me in their desire to learn, and in the effort they put forth. I think this is one of the reasons why my classes are well attended and successful.

I only wish I had more time. I'm perceptive in giving them what they need, I think. I listen to them, hear their needs, and do what I can to support them—but there never seems to be enough time, and that is often a regret.

Are there things you do every day, that you feel contribute to your successful work with families?

Yes. Pray. I pray every morning when driving to work. I ask for guidance and thank the Lord for the day.

Be prepared. I work very hard to be prepared for every day, every student.

Work to build community. I think all teachers should build community in their classroom and work at it every day. You build a community by making it a comfortable, respectable place; by having a good attitude, smiling, and making personal connections. I work very hard at building community, and it has worked for me all of the years I have taught. It is the first thing that I tell new teachers—build community.

> *"Being a family literacy educator is one of the most rewarding careers there is. It is rewarding and life changing, for both the students and for myself."*
>
> *— Patricia Urdialez*

Karen Kay Brown

Union Parish Family Literacy Center
Bernice, Louisiana

— 2010 Award Recipient —

"It's not for the child to meet your needs. You meet theirs. If you have to get out of your comfort zone, then that's your job."

— *Carolyn Taylor, Karen Kay Brown's mother*

My Habits to Share

- Be a creature of habit. A daily routine can help anyone prepare for learning.

- Say a prayer to God. Ask for a sign, if there is a life that needs you.

- Input data daily. Data keeps the doors open.

When Karen Kay Brown started working in education, she thought she was going into a career where she would work eight-to-three and be off holidays. She'd do a good job, get paid, and come home. She assumed her students wouldn't need her after school hours.

She soon learned her assumption was wrong—that her student's lives didn't stop after three o'clock in the afternoon. Their lives went on. She realized she needed to be an advocate—that she wanted to be more accessible—and that getting out of her comfort zone, was her job. Her mother was right.

Following in her mother's footsteps, and after two decades of teaching in the elementary school, Kay began to realize the great need for change at the family level, and made the transition to family literacy. Her comfort zone expanded when she started teaching adult literacy and ESL in a newly funded Even Start classroom.

> *I always knew I wanted to be a teacher. I started my career and never looked back. I love it. I want to give back to the community—put the families out there to be successful. That's my success story.*

Kay Brown has welcomed families into the Union Parish Family Literacy Center (UPFLC) and has been an integral part of its success for over a decade. During the selection year, Kay's program parents reached 100% of the main goals they set for the year, while their children met 100% of the early childhood indicators for attendance, grade promotion, and reading readiness. This national honor builds on prior local and statewide recognition earned by Kay and the Union Parish Family Literacy Center. The Louisiana Department of Education designated the center in rural Bernice, Louisiana, as one of three outstanding English Language/Civics programs in the state in 2008.

At the time of Kay's award, the UPFLC welcomed parents and their children ages birth to eight to participate in a comprehensive, four-component family literacy program. Their focuses were English as a Second Language, Civics and Citizenship, and Life Skills assistance; early childhood education; parent education; and parent-child interactive literacy activities. The UPFLC was part of the Northeast Louisiana Family Literacy Consortium, which operated 14 adult and family literacy sites in an 11-parish region of the state.

Delene W. Rawls, Ph.D., the Curriculum Coordinator at the time, stated that, "A visitor to the UPFLC will have no trouble ascertaining the mission of the staff and program. The facilities are well-equipped, and all of the staff members work as a team to integrate intergenerational literacy growth." She went on to say that, "Kay Brown and her staff are a secure team when it comes to planning and implementing high-quality activities for parents and children to learn together. Interactive literacy activities provide the rehearsal platform for new learning, for both the adult and the child." Dr. Rawls also adds, "Because fiscal and curriculum guidance are centralized, the staff members are able to focus attention on the highest-quality services to the neediest population, a job they do outstandingly well."

> *The family literacy Teacher of the Year award was a great award for me. I also received the 2013 COABE Outstanding Teacher of the Year award. I get more "rewards" however, when I see my students succeeding.*

Kay's coworkers share that her most amazing quality is that she is truly humble. "She refuses to stand alone in the limelight for the program's accomplishments, stating repeatedly that successes are the result of the larger effort of the team."

"This is not me," Kay says. "If we deserve [honor], we deserve it as a team. We work hard together."

> *I get nowhere without the team around me. This is not a one-person show.*

Today, Kay still works in the same position, coordinating the program and teaching Adult Education/ESL, and supporting families 24/7. She says she pays it forward by "investing in my home parish and in my local community, helping to make real changes beyond my classroom. I have prepared someone who can step in and have the same passion for this parish and this community in my colleague, Wendy Comfort. When I do decide to retire, I am leaving my program and my community in good hands because she can carry on the work we have started. Also, to me paying it forward is equipping my participants for a better life that will improve our community, too. Any educators in rural centers like mine can learn how to strengthen their community through the same commitment—to focus not just on this program year, but all of the future benefits possible."

This is, perhaps, but one of the reasons Kay was selected as a Toyota Teacher of the Year. When Dr. Rawls nominated Kay for the award, she wrote, "Kay believes in helping people no matter when or where or how much they need help. The ripple effect of Kay and UPFLC spreads from the participants to their extended families to the community, parish, and state, and even beyond the borders of our country. Kay Brown understands that regardless of the challenges, she must persist, leading her team to reach out, inspiring needy families toward the opportunities that await in the future."

One of Kay's greatest pleasures is sharing books with children and their parents. She has facilitated the distribution of thousands of books to at-risk children in Union Parish as part of the First Book National Book Bank Advisory Board. She has collaborated with agencies such as the Bernice Community Library to host Book Club meetings, where her adult students participated, reading such books as *The Grapes of Wrath*. She also partnered with the Louisiana Endowment for the Humanities and the Union Parish Library system to co-host PrimeTime Family Reading programs.

When Hurricane Katrina hit, Kay's first involvement with the First National Book Bank came about. They worked together to put books back into the devastated areas after the storm, rebuilding children's libraries. She says, "This project was dear to my heart. This is when I became the Louisiana Book Fairy. I hooked a U-Haul to the back of my Suburban, and with the help of my team, delivered books to children and programs in the southern part of Louisiana, about once every two weeks." At Christmastime, they gave out brand new books—that's when she says she saw "children's desperation turn to joy." Overall, they gave out close to two million books. Although she says the Louisiana Book Fairy has retired, she still takes her out to local Head Start classes occasionally, and passes out books.

It is clear that the entire community is involved in the program—from helping to recruit families to creating and managing a library for the center, because the nearest library requires transportation that many families do not have. Kay's philosophy of expanding the family to reach the entire community is paying off. And the community is reaching right back.

"Kay Brown has the remarkable ability to be motivated by the big picture while maintaining her focus on the details. She views each individual's needs for acquiring and improving literacy one at a time, not forcing them to fit a pre-determined pattern."

— Delene W. Rawls, PH.D., Curriculum Coordinator, UPFLC

In Her Own Words

Considering your work with families, what is your greatest lesson learned?

I've learned many lessons. There is no way not to learn and evolve. My biggest lesson learned, however, is how very different each family is, and what each family brings to the program. I realized that I have to be the change agent. I have to be the one willing to make that change. I always thought that every family was raised the way I was raised. Boy was I fooled. It is so not true.

When I was teaching elementary school, I had the impression that parents didn't care. But what I learned through family literacy, after I started working more closely with parents, was that it wasn't that they didn't want to help their children, they didn't have the tools they needed to work with them. That's what turned me on to family literacy. I wanted to share with them the tools that were passed along to me. That's where I needed to be the change agent.

I don't want to be untouchable. I don't want to be intimidating to the families.

My parents were always teaching. My father would get out the flashcards and go over our spelling words. My mother was an educator. I will never forget her telling me, "It's not for the child to meet your needs, it's for you to meet theirs. If you have to get out of your comfort zone, then that's your job."

If I could go back and change things, my elementary children's parents would have all of my contact information. I'd be more available. I wish I could go back and make myself more available. We provide that contact information now to our family literacy students. They know we are there 24/7.

Working with families can often be a stressful and unrewarding job. What motivates you?

My greatest success stories are my own children. Like my parents, I was very involved in their education. I see my traits coming out in them now, and in my grandchildren.

What motivates me? I love this community. It's a success when I teach about jobs and careers. I ask my students, "What's the difference between a job and a career? Can you tell me that?" A career is something you want to do long term, I tell them. Sometimes we have to do jobs in order to get to careers.

I always knew I wanted to be a teacher. I started my job with a career, and never looked back. I want to give back to the community. Putting these families out there to be successful, that's my success story.

What are some habits you have created that support you, as you support families?

First, I am a creature of habit. I get up early every morning to get a good start on the day. I stick to my routine. Even the convenience store knows my routine. I believe a daily routine can help anyone prepare for learning.

Second, I do not get out of the car every day until I say a prayer to God. I ask him every day, that if there is a life today who needs me, to please give me a sign.

And last, I input data daily. I am consumed with data and it has to be perfect. The data represents my program's outcomes and forces me to look critically at the program. Data is the key to knowing where you have come from, and where you are going. Data keeps us open.

> "The ripple effect of Kay Brown and Union Parish Family Literacy spreads from the participants to their extended families, to the community, parish, and state."

— Delene W. Rawls, PH.D., Curriculum Coordinator, Union Parish Family Literacy Center

2010

María Antonia Piñón

Riverside Elementary School
All-Aboard Family Literacy Program
Miami, Florida

──────── *2009 Award Recipient* ────────

"First of all, be yourself. See yourself not as a teacher, but as a learner. If we remain in the mindset of being a learner, we walk in their shoes. Be a learner, and grow from your own experiences, and from your students."

— *María Antonia Piñón*

──── *My Habits to Share* ────

- Ask yourself every day:
    - What have I learned today?
    - What am I grateful for today?
    - What did I do for someone else today?
- If you see a need, be pro-active.

When she was 12 years old, Maria Piñon left her native country of Cuba and migrated to the United States. She left everything behind—her friends and her home. The year was 1960, a troubling time for Cuba. Cuban-U.S. relations were growing cold, and the Cuban Revolution was drifting the country toward communism.

Once they were here, Maria's parents would say, "Even though we lost everything, we still have each other and what we have learned. Those are treasures no one can take away." From this experience, she learned the value of family and an education. She began to see education not only as a "treasure" that no one can take away, but as one to be shared.

Today, Maria makes it a practice to share her treasure chest with others. Helping adult students learn English and supporting them as they form communities of learning is her treasure chest.

English gives students the opportunities to open more doors for them.

In 2009, Maria was the supervisor of the All-Aboard Family Literacy Program in the Miami-Dade County community. The program offered a comprehensive family literacy curriculum to strengthen families, increase reading fluency, and provide important services that would benefit the community at large. The project was a collaborative effort of Riverside Elementary School; The Institute for Child and Family Health, Inc.; Sagrada Familia Head Start/Child Care Center; The Miami-Dade County Public Schools; Miami-Dade College of Early Childhood Department; Miami Behavioral Health Center; and the Miami Children's Museum. The program was designed to improve the language and literacy skills of both parents and their preschool or early school-age children and focus on improving children's school readiness and success, while simultaneously supporting the language/literacy development of the parents.

The family literacy program and its partners provided extensive services to underserved families and their children who attended a relatively low performing school. This unique public-private collaborative effort was designed to maximize the services available to the population of children and families. The comprehensive program offered five components, including early childhood preschool education, adult education (ESOL, ABE, GED), parenting education, integrated literacy activities (ILA), and a home visiting component. The model was an effective, community-based family literacy intervention.

Program Coordinator Marta Fernandez shares how Maria connected the program to the needs of the community. She says, "Maria's background helped to connect her to the families, their needs, and their goals. She, too, arrived in this country as a young child and had to learn a new language and culture. Her empathy with our families was evident in everything she did—from providing the families with bilingual dictionaries to assisting them when grocery shopping, to guiding them in their children's education, and most importantly, to encouraging them to persevere.

"Her tireless energy established partnerships with multiple agencies, individuals, and corporations within the community. Each one contributed something to the program. Whether providing workshops, field trips, or school supplies, Maria was visible at many community events. Everywhere she went she was advocating for the program and her families."

To this day, I hold the torch for whatever battles need to be fought. Family literacy is one of the battles.

Marta continues to say that today, "We are continuing Maria's legacy by dedicating our energy and resources working with Miami's most vulnerable population."

Originally a teacher and school counselor, Maria learned about a program called Even Start in the late 80s and early 90s, and eventually the school district where she worked acquired an Even Start program. She saw the changes in families and applied for the parent educator position. Over the years, Maria worked in the program, and then moved overseas. While there, she worked as a volunteer in an orphanage. When she moved back to the states, she began working in Miami for the All-Aboard program. Today, Maria has been retired for four years and lives in Texas, where she spends time with her family, helps take care of grandchildren, and volunteers at their school.

But she's not forgotten her families, and to this day, shares that, "It is heartwarming to still keep in touch with families. We formed a Facebook community and still keep in touch. The students have built friendships, and they rely on each other in many ways aside from acquiring knowledge in English and parenting. They became a close-knit community that still supports each other, including emotional support. And this is 15 years after the fact. We are all still connected—the whole family and fathers too."

Marta Fernandez adds, "I've kept in contact with some of the families and they are doing well. Our little ones are now in high school and looking forward to college. Some of the children are currently enrolled in school magnet programs and taking college preparatory classes. They have career goals of becoming oncologists, lawyers, architects, and teachers. Under Maria's guidance, the All-Aboard Family Literacy program not only encouraged these children and families to dream, but provided them with the tools to make those dreams come true."

Maria exemplified the family literacy tenet that the family is the country's smallest school. She always built on the strengths of families to help parents and children reach their goals. Under her direction, parents increased their levels of English language proficiency, obtained their GED, found employment, and became stronger, more effective supporters of their children's education.

In Maria's Own Words

How did winning the teacher of the year award influence your family education practice?

This award was very beneficial for the program, and for family literacy in the area, because it brought awareness of the need and of the good work being done. Individually, within our agency, it gave us validation. The agency more fully supported us. When no longer funded by Toyota, we were better able to secure more funds, because the award showed that "this is something that worked." The money awarded really helped out.

The families also saw the award as a source of pride, and they put out the effort to do better. The superintendent came and visited, and eventually we were provided a better facility.

What led you to this calling? What is your passion and why does it drive you?

How I was raised and the values I was given led me to this calling. My mom came from a poor family, and my father worked hard. My mother learned how to read later in life. I always saw them helping others. The fact that I loved children and knew education was so important. We need to do prevention, instead of fixing the problem after it has occurred. We do not put enough emphasis on prevention. I'm a firm believer in prevention—that is what motivated me. To this day, I hold the torch for whatever battles need to be fought. Family literacy is one of the battles.

What advice would you like to share with other teachers?

First of all, be yourself. See yourself not as a teacher but as a learner. If we remain in the mindset of being a learner, we walk in their shoes. Be a learner yourself, and learn from your own experiences and from your students.

Make sure you love what you do. You are in it because you believe it. You are in it because it is important. And you will make a difference. If not, then don't do it.

Be open to being part of the community. Let your guard down and be open to the experience. Be a part of your families' communities.

Describe three habits you have that you feel have led to your success as a family education teacher.

For the majority of my 68 years, at the end of the day, I ask myself three things:
1) What have I learned today? I have to come up with two things. If I don't, that leaves me open to look for things the next day.
2) What are two things I am grateful for today?
3) What are two things I did for someone else today?

This has helped me in my personal life and in my work life. Whether I was a teacher, counselor, supervisor, home visitor, etc. In order to think about these things at the end of the day, I had to be more aware of what I was doing all day long.

And one more thing... Never be afraid to stand up for your beliefs. If I saw a need, I was very proactive. Sometimes that got me into trouble, but I believe in going above and beyond.

> *"Under Maria's guidance, the All-Aboard Family Literacy program not only encouraged these children and families to dream, but provided them with the tools to make those dreams come true."*
>
> *— Marta Fernandez, All-Aboard Family Literacy Program Coordinator*

Katy Kibbey

Wayne Metro Community Action Agency/Even Start
Hamtramck, Michigan

2008 Award Recipient

"When my husband and I look at Ms. Katy, we seen an angel. If we have a problem, I go to her and she helps me to solve. We ask her advice a lot and she is busy, but always had time for us. I love learning and thank Ms. Katy for teaching us, to help teach the love of learning to our children."

— Taslima Nasrin, Adult Student

My Habits to Share

- Read and stay abreast of the field—continue to evolve professionally.

- Keep in touch with families—check in as often as possible.

- Advocate for families. Collect their stories.

When Katy Kibbey was teaching elementary school, she witnessed firsthand the disparity in outcomes and opportunities between students with literacy rich homes and parents, and those without. She knew then that she wanted to be part of the solution.

At the time of her award in 2008, Katy was the Even Start program director and Adult Education/ESL instructor for the Wayne Metro Even Start in Hamtramck, Michigan. In 2008, 54% of families living in Hamtramck reported English as their second language, and the Hamtramck Public Schools reported the student population represented 28 countries and 28 different primary languages. So, saying that her program served a large and diverse immigrant population would not be an understatement.

Although Katy's primary teaching responsibility was adult education, she also worked closely with the teachers of the young children. Recognizing the unique needs of the children who are second language learners, Katy established a variety of supports for learning, for both children and adults. She strived to ensure that the content of the Even Start program was relevant—full of real world materials and content.

Katy believes that intergenerational learning is one of the most powerful tools that family literacy programming offers. She states:

> *Program component integration allows parents to make connections between their learning and their children's learning. This connection has a lasting impact on the educational success of all family members.*

Katy maintains her focus on a clear goal—fostering parents' self-efficacy to be their child's first teacher. She thrives upon the success of the families she works with, and feels her adaptability is one of her strongest traits. Her classroom showed a balance of one-on-one instruction and group work. Katy leveraged partnerships with a multitude of outside organizations—intricately connecting families to the community.

In the application packet for the Teacher of the Year award, her nominator supplied the following three qualities as a rationale of her support:

"Compassionate. Katy is dedicated to her students and fellow staff, always looking for ways to recognize both small and large accomplishments. She reserves judgement and always believes in the abilities of others. When she sees an urgent need, she does everything she can to find a solution. Katy is understanding and accepting of others. This is evident to her students who develop a trust with her in spite of any cultural differences that for some would prove to be a barrier. She steps into any job at Even Start because her focus is on the families and helping her team."

"Motivational. Students and co-workers report that Katy inspires them to work harder and to achieve their goals. It is clear that her sincere belief in the abilities of others shows and serves those around her well."

"Dedicated. Katy is a tireless worker who examines each family as an individual entity with strengths and needs. She is able to incorporate differentiated learning with ease because it is something that comes naturally for her. Katy has developed her own approach for dealing with the variety of cultural differences she encounters when working in a diverse, largely immigrant community. Many people might see this as a challenge. Katy views this as an opportunity to learn and have a positive impact on families in the community. Nothing stops Katy from trying and nothing stops Katy from believing in her students and families."

Today, in 2016, Katy is still with Metro Community Action, but has moved to the director of program operations for the agency. She shares, "I am currently responsible for overseeing all agency program departments that support our agency's mission of empowering low-income individuals and strengthening communities through diverse services that address the causes and conditions of poverty. My current duties include program implementation and day-to-day operations, annual and department budgets, grant compliance, information management, and outcome monitoring, and I serve as part of the Senior Administration team reporting to the CEO."

In Her Own Words

Katy, what is your motivation for working in family literacy?

I started out my career as an elementary teacher in a poor, urban school district. As with many teachers today, I wore multiple hats to be able to assist my students with the many needs that presented on a daily basis, many of which had nothing to do with academics. When I became employed with a Community Action Agency, I was amazed to learn about so many resources available to families that would have made me a stronger teacher if I had only known. It was in Community Action and family literacy that I found the best of both worlds combined—literacy, education, and helping people transform their lives—and truly felt that I was able to make an impact and difference for the first time. I have worked with many families over the past 14 years. It is the little moments that make me reflect with gratitude on having the opportunity to serve and which remind me that the hard work and long hours are truly worth it, such as: seeing a former parent in the school halls during parent-teacher conferences; helping a former GED parent move her daughter into her college dorm at the university in which she has been awarded a full-ride; running into a parent while shopping and hearing that she is employed and her son is on the honor-roll; sitting in the audience at a community college commencement and listening to a parent who first attended our family literacy program as a shy mother learning to speak English deliver a commencement address to her fellow classmates!

How has winning the teacher of the year award influenced your family education practice?

For me, personally, it was really invigorating, because I had been teaching for eight years. I think the award kind of reignited that fire. That year was the first time I'd been to the [NCFL] conference, as well. It was an opportunity to get really good information. We were an Even Start program so a lot of our professional development was state-based, which is good training, but it was my first national exposure to other practitioners. I'm always the one who brings back and shares with my team, so the next year they had opportunities to go to the conference, as well.

At the time I got the award, I walked a dual line. I was the coordinator and the teacher, and we had other teachers. I did feel a little uncomfortable about that with my staff. I told them, "We're all getting this together. It's not just me that has this recognition."

How did your program use the award funds?

We used our funds to buy books, books, and more books. We had decided to continue to use the Mother Read model. To encourage dialogic reading, we needed book sets, one for every family, so we purchased those. At that time, we were really invested in technology, so we bought laptops and some additional cameras. I had just completed my master's in literacy, and I'd had some really good coursework around digital literacy, so I was excited to try that with our program. We did digital storybooks, and we started blogging with our families. That's how we used our funds.

Can you share a student success story?

One of our students was actually selected as an NCFL Student Speaker in 2012. She came to our program, started out as an ESL student. She was from Bangladesh and had a husband, two sons, and a daughter. She took our citizenship class and got her citizenship. She was very hungry for education, doing more for her kids. She was all about helping her children. She came into our GED program, got her GED, and is now employed with our agency in our family literacy program. Now she is taking early childhood classes at the community college.

This student completed her Associate's Degree in General Studies from Wayne Community College District. She maintained a 4.0 GPA every semester and was selected as the Student Commencement Speaker this past Saturday (6/4/16) speaking to over 2000 people at Ford Field in Detroit.

Every time I see her, she tells me how well her sons are doing. They're at the top academically in each of their grade levels, their test scores are off the charts. She is very involved.

How do you build relationships with parents?

You can have the most creative engagement activities, but nothing is more important than the relationships. Relationships have always been the key, and I think they really just develop, but you have to be intentional about developing that relationship. You have to show that you're trustworthy, that you're credible, that you're true to your word. Amongst staff, we have devoted time for planning and discussing individual families and their progress. We all have to be in this together, to best serve the family, and be on the same page.

I think too, that we create a safe environment for the families. We are generally interested in our families' cultures, as well. I think they appreciate that—at times we just go off the agenda and the plan, and just talk and share. We do home visits, too, so that's really huge for families, having us come to their homes. We show them due respect and take time to understand and value the home environment we are walking into.

I think it gives students a lot of power to know they can advocate for their child and for themselves. For me, it has always been about the relationships. I know that we have done our job well when that family comes back. When they just pop in to say, "Hello. How's it going?" I have families who still have my cell phone. They still call me. Maybe they are home for the holidays. I often pop into schools for parent-teacher conferences, and I see a family from years ago attending their child's conference. I know that we did that well. That it's keeping up.

Regarding family literacy and two-generational learning, what is the most compelling strategy you would share in terms of impact?

Our agency is very much about addressing the causes and conditions of poverty. You've changed behaviors, but you've also helped a family move up in self-sufficiency. They might not be out of poverty yet, but this generation is in a better position for the next generation. Again, for me, the impact is really told through individual stories. I can explain a program, explain what we do, and people just don't get it. When you tell a story from a family's perspective, sort of walking through what they did, how they did it, and what they accomplished, people get it.

Working with families, what is your greatest lesson learned?

My greatest lesson learned is that families can be incredibly resilient in the face of social obstacles if given the access to supportive resources beyond their immediate social network and the education around navigating the systems around such resources. My work in family literacy taught me that great and engaging lessons alone were not enough; one critical relationship with someone who truly cares about their empowerment and success, be it a staff person, family member, or friend was the key to true family empowerment.

My greatest regret has been watching investment and attention to family literacy in our state as a framework for breaking the cycle of illiteracy and poverty wane over the past years due to changing political landscapes and interests. When I started my career in family literacy, our state had over 30 Even Start Family Literacy programs. When Even Start was defunded federally at the close of 2011, we were no more than 11 programs statewide. However, this wane has made me more determined in my new role to continue to fight for family literacy, as I know firsthand that it works. This has meant being creative in finding sustainable funding, adapting program approaches, and being willing to change with the times to meet the needs of new generations of families, who are still in need of the essentials that family literacy offers.

What are three habits—things you do on a regular basis—that you feel have contributed to your successful work with families?

Continuing to evolve as a professional and leader. I continue to read and stay abreast of the field and am always on the look-out for new approaches, ways to adapt and to ultimately do better. I recognize that while my roles and responsibilities have taken me out of the front lines, I still have a unique opportunity to add value to the mission of family literacy in particular and human services in general.

Keeping in touch with families. I make a point to keep in touch with families and "check in" as much as I possibly can. To me, this is part of continuing to keep the circles of support strong.

Advocating for the needs of families. The best advocacy tools are the stories I collect by staying in touch. Data and outcomes are good; but it is the real stories of success and achievement, some of which may not happen until years after a family exits from a program, that continue to show the power of family literacy and the need for continued investment in wrapping support around the whole family—not just one member in isolation.

Gretchen White Conway

Caldwell County Even Start
Lenoir, North Carolina

—— *2007 Award Recipient* ——

"Gretchen's energy is abundant. Her eyes engage you immediately when you interact with her, and it is obvious she is focused on what you are saying. This is very reassuring to students learning English, because they recognize that she has the time to listen."

— *Student, Caldwell County Even Start*

My Habits to Share

- Listen.
- Never use "you" statements.
- Love your children!

Gretchen White Conway's career began in 1981 in Wichita, Kansas, where she fell in love with working with young children with disabilities and their families. Teaching, however, was not the career she set out to have. "I have to laugh about my story...teaching is not what I expected to do," she shares, "although as I child I loved to pretend I was the teacher using the side of my dresser as a chalkboard. I was going to be an actress! I majored in Speech and Drama in college with an Elementary Education degree as a backup. I tried my hand at acting, but was just too shy during all those auditions. I even went to Hollywood to audition for the movie *Jesus Christ Superstar*, but I guess God had a different path for me.

"I started a job as a preschool special education teacher and decided to go back to college for my Master's. I fell in love with the children. They were fun, they were funny, and they had so much potential I knew I had found a place for my acting talents—since we all know we all need a bit of acting and comedy in us to teach! So from there, teaching has taken me in so many directions: preschool teacher, college instructor, second grade teacher (for one year), and back to preschool. My love has always been being a child's second teacher, as parents will always be their child's first teacher. Teaching young children is so rewarding in many ways, and I never turn down the hugs!"

> *Embracing those moments when parents share their celebrations and heartaches is how we effectively teach. I feel like I am a better person and educator by listening more to my parents and judging less.*

Gretchen White Conway earned her B.A. from Kansas Wesleyan University majoring in Elementary Education and Theatre Arts, with a minor in English and Music; and an M.Ed. at Wichita State University in Educational Psychology/Early Childhood Special Education. Her teaching career started in 1981 in Wichita, Kansas, where she fell in love working with young children with disabilities and their families. Gretchen worked for early childhood programs in Kansas and in Arizona on the Colorado River Indian Tribe Reservation with children from four Indian tribes and migrant Mexican families, before teaching in North Carolina. On the reservation, she was also a CDA instructor to teachers and parents, who became teacher assistants.

In Kansas, she was a Practicum Coordinator and instructor for pre-special education teachers at a college consortium, Associated Colleges of Central Kansas (ACCK), and co-developed a curriculum, Navigating the Resource Maze. In North Carolina, she served as the Early Childhood Coordinator for the Caldwell County Even Start Family Literacy program. As a child advocate, she served on the North Carolina Infant/Toddler Guidelines Committee.

Under her leadership, the Caldwell County Even Start program achieved the highest ratings of its North Carolina voluntary higher standards rated license and also received exceptional scores on the Infant/Toddler and Early Childhood Environmental Rating Scales.

Gretchen worked closely with the adult education instructor at Caldwell to coordinate curricula and determine how the adult and children's components were integrated. She coordinated the early childhood components at two locations and was often seen in the children's classrooms playing on the floor with children. Everyone knew Gretchen would stop whatever she was doing to help out in anyone's classroom. Although her classroom work focused on early childhood, her ability to work with and reassure parents as learners was reflected in a 94% retention rate. She realized that encouraging adult persistence was "key" to program stability.

Today, Gretchen is still teaching in the same district where she received her award, but the program is no longer funded through Family Literacy/Even Start. Gretchen shares that, "Gamewell Elementary School, Lenoir, North Carolina, is where my classroom is now, and I love being a part of a school setting. What I miss the most about not being with Family Literacy are the parents. Even though I still get to interact with parents during drop off and pick up, it's just not the same connection you get during PACT Time and home visits. In fact, just this year we have been discussing with our program administrators about adding more parent involvement and home visiting. I am excited for that to become a reality."

Gretchen participates in long-range planning for the preschool programs within the school district. She enjoys facilitating children's learning, supporting parents' goals, and being a part of a large family of learners.

In Her Own Words

What is your greatest lesson learned working with families?

My greatest lesson learned from working with families is that they are just like me. They have their successes, their failures, their happiness, their sadness, but most of all they have their love for their children and desire to provide the best for them.

Is there anything you've done, that you would do differently now?

Oh my! My greatest failure was before I had children of my own. I think most educators can agree with me here. The expectations I had of parents and the way I judged parents for not seeing my way of thinking. I laugh about it now, but I also feel a bit ashamed. Parents are not perfect, as I know since I too am a parent. Time, money, emotions can all affect how we parent, and judging parents because of those things is not the way to effectively teach. Embracing those moments when parents share their celebrations and heartaches is how we effectively teach. I feel like I am a better person and educator by listening more to my parents and judging less.

Do you ever pay it forward?

I do not have a "pay it forward" activity per se, but when I see a child in my care needing for something, shoes, clothes, coat...somehow it will appear in their cubby. My mother always told me that what I do for my children and their parents will never be forgotten, and I pray that they will use that and "pay it forward" through their children.

What three habits do you possess that may have contributed to your successful work with families?

Listen. Take time to listen to parents.

Never use "you" statements. That causes judging and will turn a parent off from hearing anything you say.

Love their child! Always show a parent that you love their child "almost" as much as they do.

> *"My greatest lesson learned from working with families is that they are just like me. They have their successes, their failures, their happiness, their sadness, but most of all they have their love for their children and desire to provide the best for them."*
>
> — *Gretchen White Conway, Caldwell County Even Start*

Mark Faloni

Even Start Multicultural Family Literacy Program at Bancroft
and Mary's Center (now Briya Charter School)
Washington, DC

2006 Award Recipient

"[Mark's] dynamic, participatory teaching style motivates students to continue learning. His use of humor, dramatizations, and personal stories creates a bond with students who not only relate to him as a teacher, but also identify with him as a parent. This connection is powerful."

— *Christie McKay, Program Director*

My Habits to Share

- Be informed and prepared. Give students the best possible quality of classes that you can deliver.
- Be genuine, fair, and honest with students. Tell them what they did well, what they didn't do so well, and what they need to work on to get better.
- Don't get mad or upset, but be truthful. Students appreciate that "realness."

After 25 years of teaching in the same classroom, and well over 6,000 commutes from home to school, Mark Faloni's philosophy of teaching remains the same:

> *I get to teach my students English and the American culture, and they get to teach me life.*

This reciprocity of teaching and learning is clearly demonstrated by Mark's sincere viewpoint of working with his students. "I am honored and humbled to learn as much as I do from them about the richness of their cultures, traditions, and lives. I always tell them that the closest I am probably ever going to get to Burkina Faso, Uzbekistan, or Chirilagua, El Salvador is through learning about their stories and customs. I never got into this profession to 'help the downtrodden or fix the burdened.' I don't look at it this way at all. I am here to celebrate their full and already successful lives. I am only here to take them from wherever they are when they come in, move them forward, and crack open the door of opportunity. They can burst the door open and run through it to even more success. I like nothing better than hearing a success story from a student in my current class, who tells me about a student I taught 10 or 15 years ago, who is now doing great things (and there are many). It is rewarding to think that maybe I had a tiny part in that success."

> *My students have a lot to offer. I learn way more than they learn, probably, because the closest I am ever going to get to their countries is through the people sitting in my classroom. We're all learning together.*

Mark is one of the founders of the Even Start Multicultural Family Literacy Program in Washington, DC. Even Start Multicultural began in 1989 as one of the first Even Start Pilot programs with DC Public Schools. At the time of Mark's award in 2006, the program had forged collaborative partnership efforts with Bancroft Elementary School, DC Public Schools Head Start, and Mary's Center for Maternal and Child Care. Aimed to alleviate the cycle of poverty and illiteracy, the program delivered multiple levels of family literacy classes at Bancroft and Mary's Center and provided both parents and children the necessary skills to be successful participants in society. Today, the program has become a family literacy charter school, Briya Public Charter School.

An adult education and English as a Second Language (ESL) teacher with the program, Mark holds a Bachelor of Arts degree in Spanish from Washington College and a Master's Degree in Adult Education from George Mason University. Mark developed curriculum for his Intermediate II and Advanced ESL classes, aligned with Equipped for the Future and CASAS Competencies, and incorporated student interests and skills needed to accomplish their goals. His teaching responsibilities also went beyond the academic, as Mark played a primary role in teaching culturally appropriate parent education and Parent and Child Together (PACT) Time® classes.

> *Having been here so long lends itself to a trust and rapport that I can build with the new students, who find out that I have been doing this for all these years. This experience is comforting to them and they learn to trust that I have their best interest at heart.*

Program Director, Christie McKay shares that "Mark recognized the importance of families reading together more and increasing their access to books. He provided leadership in his team while planning the PACT Time preschool lessons with a strong literacy focus." Concerning teaching parent education, she adds that Mark "brought to life the classes with his personal experience and anecdotes about his own family. He is able to sympathize and bond with parents, as well as share effective parent techniques he has implemented at home."

Mark says, "I try to be informed and prepared, so I can give the students the best possible quality of classes I can deliver. I want them to be interesting, informative, lively, and engaging." He doesn't view himself as the typical ESL teacher. "I played two college sports and I am much more of a coach-type teacher than the stereotypical, bubbly ESL teacher, where everything is great and lovely all the time. Instead, I tell them what they did well, what they didn't do so well, and what they need to work on to get better in the total language acquisition, and then we work on those things." He adds that his students know that he won't get mad or upset. "I am truthful and they appreciate that 'realness'."

> *I am genuine, fair, and honest with students. I tell them what they did well, what they didn't do so well, and what they need to work on to get better.*

When asked what is his greatest lesson learned working with families, Mark states the following. "I guess it is both a lesson learned and a validation of what I thought when I got into this business in 1990—99.9% of all the thousands (literally) of families I have worked with over the years all have the same basic needs, wants, and dreams for the people they love and care about. Most immigrated here for a myriad of reasons, from escaping war-torn areas, to better jobs, schools, and opportunities for their families. They all are interested in learning English, understanding how Americans think and act, and how to get along in their own neighborhoods. They have all sacrificed a lot—foregoing family, friends, language, cultural connections, and family support systems, etc.—in order to make better lives for themselves and their children. It doesn't really matter what headscarf they wear or what language they speak or what God they believe in; they all want to be confident, successful, healthy, and happy. That's what I love about this job. I can teach them the English they need, which eventually leads to confidence and self-advocacy. I am honored to see the total human growth of the individual and it is astounding!"

> *They learn English, and English builds confidence, and education builds power.*

In a focus group of Teacher of the Year award recipients who met at NCFL's Family Learning Summit 2015, Mark shared a success story of one of his students that represents the type of growth many of his students have achieved. One of the first students in the Even Start program was a young Vietnamese woman with a one-year-old daughter. "She was a good student," Mark said. "Didn't know English so she learned. You could see she was a real go-getter, a worker. She eventually learned English and we hired her, because we thought she could reach out to the Vietnamese community. Next thing she says, 'I want to go and work in the school.' She left us and got her Bachelor's degree from the University of DC. Time went on, and she earned her Master's degree from George Mason. Her little daughter eventually went to the University of Maryland, and now teaches in the same school with her mom, where they started out in our program."

In His Own Words

Mark, what are your thoughts about the partnerships that support this award?

The one thing the grant money brought in for us was an infant and toddler class. Securing funding for that particular age is tougher than getting preschool funding in DC.

The other thing is recognition. Our particular site had two Toyota Teacher of the Year award winners in three years. That was big as far as recognition, and for funders to be able to say, "This site has two of the last three or four (teachers of the year)." That recognition was more awareness for people interested in potentially funding us. Maybe it meant we're doing good work because of it.

What's really great about both organizations (Toyota and NCFL) is that they seem to be in this for the long haul, and it's sustained. To me, that is really important. I see Toyota as a sustained partner. They chose to champion this cause and I think that is great. The same with NCFL.

NCFL has been at this for a long time, as I understand. I think this is really neat because it kind of validates what we've been doing, especially when we go to (NCFL conference) breakout sessions and hear people across the country giving feedback. I think, "That's really good. That's what we've been doing for a long time and it seems to be working very well." I think that the length of time NCFL is willing to be involved is a great thing.

You obviously have a good working relationship with your students. How do you build parent-to-parent support? How do you set the stage for that?

Our program is very learner centered. It's their program. They take ownership of it and when things are relevant to their lives and meaningful, they are much more engaged. The trust level is huge in our program because we are getting people who are recent immigrants. That's a big step. It's a huge and scary step. Students find the program and they feel like, "Wow, these people. They're not condescending, they are trust building. They say we're going to work with you from where you came in."

My class is an English class. Yeah, it's grammar, but it's so much more than that. It's a wealth of knowledge from people all over the world. Before you know it, everybody is chiming in and helping each other, and they get friends out of it. They realize they are all in the same situation together. Of course, they learn English, and English builds confidence, and education builds power—but watching the students burst out of their shells is rewarding.

My greatest regret is that I am not able to help the students as much as I would like, but this might also not be such a bad thing. Helping too much or handholding through difficult situations and bureaucratic red tape might prohibit growth and empowerment of the students. They may need initial help or a phone call made for them, but eventually they are going to have to go and do.

We try to let it go and say, "Now you've got the power. You're allowed to do this. You can speak up and have a voice." Next thing you know, a parent in the class is now the PTA president. To me, that's the biggest thing—the confidence level and the sharing in class, so that people get friends and classmates. People they can trust.

You make this sound like it just happens. How do you do this?

I think the biggest thing is that my students see me as a person who has their best interest at heart. What I tell them is, "There are two things I have that you don't have. I have the English language I can convey. I can help you with that. And, I have the understanding of the society of the American culture." That's the only difference. I tell them what they are going to get from me, but then all of these other things are happening, too.

The students start to realize that I'm going to treat them like a person. That we're going to discuss, and the class is going to get loud, and we're going to disagree sometimes, and we're going to talk about things that might be a little controversial. Things that are happening in our lives. And they feel comfortable.

I get totally rewarded when all of a sudden a student tells something very serious and private in front of the whole class, and to me—this white male teacher from Baltimore who is totally unlike them, my immigrant women students—and that is just amazing. To me, that's when the trust is so high they've decided, "I'm going to tell you this." My class—sometimes it's an English class, sometimes it's group therapy.

> *"In a city where people don't seem to have the time to stop and listen, Mark takes the time to get to know his students' culture, families, and dreams to create a classroom of hope."*
>
> ~ *Christy McKay, Program Director*

——— 2006 ———

Amy Hall

Hannahville Family and Child Education (FACE) Program
Wilson, Michigan

2005 Award Recipient

"Miss Amy spends her time listening and teaching…with much patience and a huge smile. I sometimes wonder if she ever gets tired. She makes sure that every preschooler is safe and happy."

— Shelli Feathers, former FACE Student

My Habits to Share

- Negative behavior is an opportunity to remind yourself that children and adults walk in the door every day with challenges. Be part of their successes.

- No child or parent is a cookie cutter. Support each person individually. Remembering this allows you to stay fresh and grow as an educator.

- Trust is important.

On any typical school day, Amy Hall is the first of her staff members to arrive at school. She comes in early, with one basic purpose in mind—to make sure she greets each child and parent upon arrival. This simple gesture is one of the many reasons why Amy was chosen for the Toyota Teacher of the Year award in 2005.

> *I see my role as an advocate for children and parents, affirming them and instilling the "I can do anything" attitude.*

During her sixth year of teaching in the Hannahville Family and Child Education (FACE) program, Amy was nominated for, and received, the Toyota Teacher of the Year award. As the preschool teacher in the four-component family literacy program, she taught a multi-level classroom that consisted of children ages three years to those ready to enter kindergarten.

The Hannahville FACE program is a two-generational family literacy program in operation since 1992 at the Hannahville Indian School. Located in the Hannahville Indian Community in Michigan's Upper Peninsula, the school was established in 1976 to address the special academic needs of Potawatomi students while teaching them about their history and culture. The school started as a K-8 single classroom and has grown to include students grades K-12, with elementary and high school wings, plus industrial arts, adult education, preschool and child care offerings. According to the school website, "the child care center and FACE Program have been valuable assets to the community, encouraging more participation in adult education and college programs by young parents."

> *FACE is unique in that it is culturally significant. What has worked for me is viewing the program in a place where "we are all one, and we treat others as they want to be treated." This fits despite culture.*

Amy holds a Bachelor's Degree with teacher certification in Child Care, Family Life Education, and Home Economics. Prior to her work with FACE, she was the coordinator of the local Early On program, which provided early intervention services to the local Indian community. Former FACE Coordinator and Hannahville School Principal Rose Potvin described Amy's work in the Early On program as an important partnership, which eventually led her to work with FACE. Rose shared that as Amy "advocated for our community and built on our strengths, we became more confident and better able to meet the needs of our families. When someone else tells you strongly enough that you are important, you begin to believe it, and others do also."

The FACE program maintained the traditional four-component model of family literacy designed by NCFL—Adult Education, Early Childhood Education, Parent Time, and PACT (Parent and Child Together) Time—for many years. In 2014, the program, funded by the Bureau of Indian Education (BIE), shifted its guidelines to accommodate fewer hours of on-site participation for parents. As a result, Amy shares, "We are experiencing many new adventures with our families. We are rich with staff and are moving forward after some departures. Our parents are diverse, we have three experiencing college, one incarcerated, several in treatment, two homeless, and two that have obtained employment already this month. We have an array of documentation avenues (for parent involvement). I believe the flex and partial participation of parents is more family friendly, but I find it more challenging to individualize the instruction, document, and assess."

Challenges do not stop Amy in her tracks, however. She views challenge as an opportunity.

> *When I see a negative behavior, it is an opportunity to remind myself that children and adults walk in the door each day with different challenges, and I want to be part of their successes.*

"FACE is a strengths model," shares Rose Potvin. "Amy exemplifies that in everything she does. She has a rare gift of bringing out the best in everyone she comes in contact with, both personally and professionally. Through her quiet influence and support, Amy brings out the strengths in all of us."

The retention of families has always been a priority for Amy. If a family failed to show up at school, she would conduct a home visit, bring an activity for the child, let the parents know how much they were missed, and that supports were available at school.

> *Every day I try to be mindful of paying it forward. We are a dependent society and we don't make it alone. I have this in the back of my mind daily. When you see the gratitude, and it's being passed along, it's even more powerful.*

One of Amy's former students shares, "There was a time when I was going to drop out of school and Miss Amy showed up at my house and talked to me about the problem I was having. She told me I'd come too far to stop now, and she was right. She made me realize I couldn't give up on my goals. Amy comes down to the adult education room every morning and talks to us, and asks if there is anything we need or if we just need to talk. She goes over our goals that we have set for the end of the year, and she makes sure we don't fall off track too much. There was a day I was running late for school and Amy drove all the way back into town to see if anything was wrong. I got to school and Miss Christy told me that Amy was going to my house to check on me. You don't see this kind of kindness very often."

Eleven years after the Teacher of the Year honor, and after 18 years of working in the Hannahville FACE program, Amy is still very much involved working with families. A few years ago, she traded her preschool teacher hat to work more closely with the adults in the adult education classroom.

> *I'm still doing family literacy today and loving it. It works. Coming from a diverse background of working with families, adults, and children, I really buy in to the family literacy model.*

Her job title may have changed, but her daily focus is still on families. Comfortable stepping into the adult education teacher role, Amy knows that parents are children's best teachers, and that parent engagement is the key to children's success. New administration in the Hannahville School has brought a stronger focus on collaboration with other early childhood programs in the community and the potential to serve more families. With the changes brought about from the BIE for adult education and parent involvement, Amy works to reinvent her role with parents and families to focus more largely on supporting high-quality parent engagement.

"I met Miss Amy and she seemed so encouraging and supportive. She told me that I would be able to get my diploma or GED and I could have day care arranged so I wouldn't have to be away from my child too long. Then, Miss Amy showed me all of the different FACE rooms and how important children and family are to this program. I was told they understand that family is the number one priority. We talked for a little while and I left feeling much better about the new school year. I felt relieved about the situation." When asked how to set the stage to build this kind of parent support, Amy replied,

> *You create a community where you build trust. Then step back and it happens.*

She also says you have to listen. That both early childhood and adult education teachers should know their students and their goals. In addition, "when teachers foster support for their students' goals, amazing things can happen." She adds, "I find it exciting when we set weekly goals in our program. The parents create a natural parent-to-parent network of support, and they are encouraging the other students. When that trust level builds, then they are supporting each other. To step back and watch that parent-to-parent support—whether they are going off to college, or taking a GED test, or an entrance exam; whether it's academic or for their children—is, I think, priceless."

After 18 years of working intensively with families, it's easy to wonder what drives a teacher like Amy. She says, "It's very basic. It's not traditional school. Each day is different because of the families we serve, and it stays very engaging. What drives me is that I see a need. I see the importance of the big picture, but the day-to-day is fun and enjoyable. I'd be lying if I said it wasn't demanding and hard work, but after all the years, it's good work. For me, it's a real fit. I think of my own personal story. I came from a family where my grandfather was illiterate. I didn't know that growing up. But he raised nine children and was successful and happy, and his children even more so. It's a dual journey, parents and children together."

It is important to follow guidelines and policies and comply, but when it comes to crunch time and I need to make a decision, I focus on the family first.

In Her Own Words

How has winning the teacher of the year award influenced your family education practice?

Winning the award helped to mold me as a teacher for sure, and even my life. I feel I'm part of a larger circle now. It's like an extended family. Toyota has been very quiet in our support, just like the Prius. It's moving us forward, but in a quiet way. I believe the smaller the community, the greater the impact of this award. I look at it like a program gift.

We used the program funds from the award for gap services, to supplement funds not in the budget, and allow for more meaningful family engagement experiences. Being in a very rural area between two counties, when we do have family events, there is a need for more support for families to attend. That was one part of the distribution. Another was technology. We have two Smart Boards in our classrooms now, one in early childhood and the other in adult education. To be able to parallel the parents' learning with what the children are learning is phenomenal. Technology has opened our world. The winters are long, but we're able to travel with *Wonderopolis*®, and the other apps. The children are fluent with the technology, so that's exciting.

Our circle is made bigger by strong partners. It allows us to give to the families and the families to give to the community.

We often have visitors and showcase our program and the collective strengths we bring as a team. Someone else may point out that I was Toyota Teacher of the Year. It's a source of pride for the community, for our program, for the tribe, for my family. I guess we encourage and invite the community to come and to partner, and be a part of it. We open it up.

The partnership between our school, Toyota, and NCFL has encompassed a whole group of individuals. When our circle is made bigger by strong partners, it allows us to give to the families and the families to give to the community. To me, that's just a real natural family engagement step. It puts parents and the families at the table, which allows children to be at the table when it's time to start school.

Having the support from NCFL is like being from a strong family. When we're in the school, working day to day, it's just like having a real, strong family.

"Her job is not just professional. She also takes an interest in the families with whom she is involved. You can easily see that she wants the best for them and hopes that each family will turn out to be a success. We need teachers that care the way Miss Amy does."

— Shelli Feathers, former FACE Student

——— 2005 ———

Lorie Preheim

Even Start Multicultural Family Literacy Program
Mary's Center for Maternal and Child Care, Inc.
(now Briya Charter School)
Washington, DC

─── **2004 Award Recipient** ───

"The most important qualities Lorie brings to family literacy are love and compassion for her students and teaching."

— *Christie McKay, Program Director*

My Habits to Share

- Use a positive approach by looking for the good in everything.
- Be passionate and enthusiastic about your work.
- Treat everyone equally and with respect.

From spending several years as a young girl in Africa, to working with children in the streets of Bolivia, to teaching ESL instruction in an Even Start program in Washington, DC, Lorie Preheim's multicultural experiences are vast, and her dedication to children, families, and family literacy goes far beyond the classroom.

Even Start Director, Christie McKay, shares that, "Ms. Preheim is a very dynamic teacher. She uses all kinds of activities to keep her students motivated to continue learning. Her students love her because she is willing to go the extra mile to help them find employment, to assist them with medical appointments, to counsel them on their family's problems. She always has time after class to listen and try to help."

> *The most powerful learning environment happens when we, as teachers, share from our personal experiences and talk about our struggles, insights, and successes as parents, workers, community members, and ourselves. When you share your own difficulties, it allows for a more open conversation where the adult students don't feel judged.*

The mission of the Even Start Multicultural Family Literacy program was to serve those most in need by providing quality educational opportunities for both parents and their children ages birth to five years, in a multi-generational setting. Even Start Multicultural began in 1989 as one of the first Even Start pilot programs with DC Public Schools. At the time of Lorie's award, it was a collaborative effort of Bancroft Elementary School, DC Public Schools and Head Start, and Mary's Center for Maternal and Child Care (the lead and fiscal agent). Even Start Multicultural conducted multiple levels of family literacy classes at Bancroft Elementary School and Mary's Center. The program aimed to alleviate the cycle of poverty and illiteracy by giving both parents and children necessary skills to be successful participants in society. The program increases the literacy levels and job skills of immigrant parents, helping them gain skills to be full partners in their child's education.

Today, Lorie Preheim is Briya Public Charter School's Academic Dean and charter school founder. She has been with the school for 18 years and has 24 years of experience in the field of adult education and family literacy. Lorie earned a Master's degree in Adult Education: Curriculum & Instruction with a specialization in learning disabilities at George Mason University and a B.A. in Education, International Development, and Art at Bethel College. She sits on the Adult Education Performance Management Framework task force for the DC Public Charter School Board. She has been Board President for the Learning Disabilities Association DC Chapter and has continued to volunteer for the organization since 2005.

Lorie shares, "I have continued to work at the same school in different capacities over the years. During my time as Academic Dean, I have been responsible for items such as program development, professional development for instructors and staff, developing and revising the curriculum to incorporate best practices, ensuring the learners meet academic learning gains, grant writing, staff hiring and orientation, supervision, enrollment, outreach, facilities design, and expansion of the school to four sites. Recently, I have been working on expanding our workforce development course offerings including starting a new Medical Assistant Program. I am on the Briya management team and DC Public Charter School Board adult education performance management framework task force. Finally, I work with CASAS (California Adult Student Assessment System) to review their test item development for the new reading assessment which will integrate the College and Career Readiness Standards for Adult Education. I have also helped CASAS develop the Functional Writing Assessment training materials and have reviewed test items for the Listening assessment.

In Her Own Words

What is your greatest lesson learned working with families?

The greatest lesson I have learned is that the most powerful learning environment happens when we as teachers share from our personal experiences and talk about our struggles, insights, and successes as parents, workers, community members, and ourselves. When you share your own difficulties, it allows for a more open conversation where the adult students don't feel judged. Students learn that it is okay to make mistakes, and it is okay to try something and have it not work. We learn as much from what doesn't work as from what does work. When we recognized that parenting is difficult and every child responds differently, we get more honest, open sharing. This creates a safe environment where everyone can share and learn from each other's experiences.

Once I was sharing with my class how my 2 ½ year old almost broke down her bedroom door when I was trying the Magic 1, 2, 3 technique. We had a few weeks of screaming and tantrums at the bedroom door before she learned that when we get to 3, she needs to make a good choice or she will go in timeout. She did finally learn and from that point forward, my life as a parent was radically easier. When I started counting, by the time I got to 2, she would make good choices and do what was expected. The Magic didn't work without a little sweat and tears first. Sharing my own experience has made others feel comfortable to share their own tests and trials of parenting and has helped them gain the inner strength and patience when working with their own children.

What is your greatest regret/failure, and how did it make you do or see things differently?

I remember one student, Maria, who really struggled in the classroom. She participated in our school for several years, but her attendance was very sporadic and thus her progress was very limited. She worked so it was not unusual for her to miss 2-4 days a week. She was eager and interested but sometimes got the wide-eyed look of being lost or overwhelmed. Missing a lot of class did not help.

Looking back, I wish I knew then what I know now. If I could have her in my classroom again, I would provide her with more explicit instruction incorporating chunking, repetition of information and vocabulary, differentiated instruction, and scaffolding. I would also have her assessed for learning disabilities. I wonder if I had been able to provide her more targeted instruction with clear objectives and manageable steps that met her individual needs maybe she would have come more frequently and made more progress.

My best teacher happened to be my high school teacher, Ms. Olais. She gave me the overall framework and structure of the class from the beginning. She laid out what I needed to do to succeed and what the expectations were for work completed to get an A, B, or C. The goals were clearly defined and she provided the instruction, tools, time, and space to meet the expectations. I knew the path and how to get there from the beginning. Each student determined at what level they wanted to perform according to how much time and effort they wanted to put in. I knew where I was going and how I could get there. She also provided clear instruction with lots of modeling, visuals, practice, and reflective dialogue about our work. We did projects, which highly motivated me. The projects had the right amount of student-led decisions and teacher requirements incorporating skills and competencies to be gained throughout the project. To this day, I still model my teaching after this one amazing teacher who so influenced my life and my profession as a teacher.

What motivates you, day in and day out? What inspires you to work with families?

I grew up around people from all over the world. My father worked in International Development and we lived in Africa when I was 3-5 years old. This had a great impact on my interest in working with people from around the world. Our house was full of artwork from Africa and Asia. My dad travelled abroad 50% of the time and would come home with artifacts from other countries. This peaked my curiosity. I have always been drawn to learn about people and cultures different from my own. I love discovering how we are similar and how we are different, including anything from the foods we eat, the vocabulary we use, how we live, our values, and our concepts of community and religion.

I am passionate about making human connections and bridging cultures through interacting in a meaningful way, having conversations, and making friendships. Building relationships across cultures is a powerful tool in bringing about peace and social justice in the world. That one-on-one contact is invaluable in gaining a better understanding of each other. It breaks down barriers, stereotypes, misconceptions, and fear. It builds friendship, love, caring, connections, and kindness. We can do all that in our classrooms through group projects, interactive activities, classroom assignments, and social and cultural events. The environment the teacher creates and the opportunity to share and learn from each other is powerful.

We can make change and impact the world through education right here in the United States in our 400 square foot classrooms.

How do you pay it forward?

My favorite teachers, whom I still use as role models in education to this day, were the ones who took the time to get to know me personally. They called me by my first name, reached out to me, listened to me, respected me, and treated me like an equal even though at the time I was significantly younger. They were also flexible and understanding of my individual needs. Throughout my career, I've tried to pay that forward by making time before, during, and after class or work to answer any questions and support others in any way I can. When you help people with little, medium, and big problems by listening to their concerns, discussing options, and linking them to resources that make their lives more manageable without judging them, they feel supported and empowered. With colleagues, this can be achieved by providing a flexible supportive space where you can learn by doing, pilot new ideas, and adjust practices as needed. There is no such thing as failure. Any experience is a success because you learn from it and make a positive change as a result.

Name three "habits" or things you do on a regular basis you feel may have contributed to your successful support of families over the years.

I make a habit of using a positive approach. By looking for the good in everything whether it be people, staff's talents, materials, professional development and seeing how that can support and improve the work, you create a positive environment with continuous program improvement. Looking for new information and integrating new concepts and best practices into curriculum, instruction, and assessment keeps the work current and effective. Looking for how staff's skills and interests can benefit the school keeps the staff enthusiastic, motivated, and dedicated to meeting the learners' needs.

I make a habit of being passionate and enthusiastic about my work. Excitement and energy about projects, new initiatives, and simple to difficult tasks is contagious. It draws others in and generates more creative energy.

I make a habit of treating everyone equally and with respect. I treat the CEO, the Basic I student, and the maintenance staff equally. Everyone is valued equally. Everyone feels equally important and a part of the greater whole. We all make a difference and we all contribute to the success of the school.

> *"This nomination focuses on the skills, research, and academic knowledge Ms. Preheim brings to her classroom, but the most important qualities she brings to family literacy is her love and compassion for her students and teaching."*
>
> *— Christie McKay, Program Director*

───── **2004** ─────

Jody Lintzenich

Haywood Elementary School
Nashville, Tennessee

2003 Award Recipient

"She empowers and energizes the family literacy program through adventure and education. Jody has proven there is a way to develop a rewarding program that has something for everyone."

— *Donnetta McKissack, Literacy Coordinator, Haywood Elementary*

My Habits to Share

- Try new things. See challenge as an opportunity.
- Treat families like family. Make them feel comfortable.
- Set goals and work to achieve them. Every day is a new opportunity.

Jody Lintzenich always felt she had a rapport with children, so teaching was a natural fit. After several years of teaching early elementary grades, she earned a master's degree in Teaching English as a Second Language (ESL), and soon thereafter, began her work in family literacy—working with the Toyota Families in Schools program.

Jody was a family literacy educator at Haywood Elementary School in Nashville-Davidson County, Tennessee, at the time of her award in 2003. She had spent 25 years in education, 13 of those years teaching children and parents at Haywood. She created the family literacy program at Haywood, extending her desire to reach the parents of the children she taught. According to her nominating application, Jody "reached the overall school parent population by organizing affordable book fairs and literacy festivals, often driving around the state to pick up free books for these events. Her days were filled with teaching 250 students English as a Second Language, and her nights were filled with managing the Toyota Family Literacy Program.

> *Inspiring children to be all that they can be is "paying it forward" because they in turn will do that for someone else.*

According to Donetta McKissack, Literacy Coordinator at Haywood, "Jody has definitely made an impact on our children and adults with outstanding development and experience throughout the years. She empowers and energizes the family literacy program through adventure and education. Jody has proven that there is a way to develop a rewarding program that has something for everyone."

Today, Jody has technically "retired," but it is difficult to keep her out of the classroom. She says, "I am not still working at Haywood Elementary. For the 2003/04 year, I transferred to Whitsitt Elementary where I taught 2nd grade for three years and 3rd grade for nine years. I retired from Metro Nashville Public Schools in May of 2015. For the 2015/16 school year, I had a 120-day contract at Maxwell Elementary where I worked with small groups of children helping them improve their reading and math skills.

> *What drives me is the fact that I need a purpose. If I can change the future of children, that is my driving force and passion. I have always worked hard—I was instilled with a strong work ethic when I was a child—and I have never lost that.*

In Her Own Words

Jody, you've worked with children and families for many years. What is your greatest lesson learned?

I've learned that all families—no matter what nationality—want a better life for their children and they believe education is the key. Even though the parents didn't know the language and couldn't help the children with their homework, they wanted their children to succeed in school.

Sometimes we experience failures, or wish we had done things differently. Looking back, would you do anything differently?

I don't use the word "failure" and do not consider anything I have done a "failure." Working with the families, I planned a lot of lessons and events. Due to lessons learned, I re-evaluated and changed things from year to year to improve the activity, but never thought of what we did as a "failure." I believe a good educator constantly reevaluates and makes adjustments according to what worked, what didn't, and what improvements could be made.

What's your story? What motivates you every day?

In 1990, I received a call from central office at Metro Nashville Public Schools, the day before school started, telling me I was not to return to my previous school as they needed to lose a teacher—and I was that teacher. I was sent to Haywood Elementary to teach 26 little first graders. That move—an unwelcome surprise at the time—turned out to be the best thing that happened to me. After working there several years, the ESL teacher came to me one day and told me Metro would be expanding their ESL program and thought I would be a good teacher for ESL children. She thought I should get my certification, so I went to Carson Newman and got a master's degree in TESOL. My position at Haywood changed and I worked only with ESL students. After that, I was given the opportunity to be a part of the Toyota Families in Schools program that was going to be at Haywood. Working with the families was a true joy. I worked day and night for several years—teaching students by day and working with families at night. In 1997, I attended the NCFL convention in Louisville. I was inspired by the Teacher of the Year and decided that was the goal I needed to work toward. In 2003 that goal became reality.

Even though I transferred from Haywood, I never stopped working with ESL children. I saw how eager they were to learn and saw how much progress they made. Education has changed over the years and I made the decision to retire in 2015. Even though I was retiring, I knew I was not ready to stop teaching, so I found a job teaching children reading and math skills —the majority ESL students.

What drives me is the fact that I need a purpose. If I can change the future of children, that is my driving force and passion. I have always worked hard—I was instilled with a strong work ethic when I was a child—and I have never lost that.

Every change that I have made in my educational career has been the right one for me at that time. Currently I work at Maxwell Elementary and truly love what I do. Knowing I am making a difference in the lives of children is what keeps me getting up each morning and arriving at school by 7:45 a.m.

How do you pay it forward?

I believe that teaching children to read is "paying it forward." Once children can read, they can do anything. For example, a little first grader I worked with in class and literacy just graduated from college last year with a degree in special education. She will in turn be teaching children. Inspiring children to be all that they can be is "paying it forward" because they in turn will do that for someone else.

Name three things you do on a regular basis that you feel may have contributed to your successful work with families.

I am not afraid to try new things. I see it as a challenge. I knew nothing about family literacy when I was approached with the opportunity, but decided I would stretch myself and learn something new.

I treated the families in my program as if they were my family. I worked tirelessly to give them a good experience and help them to succeed. I used my gift of hospitality as I prepared homemade snacks for each class. I tried to make each person feel comfortable coming to the program.

I set goals and work hard to achieve those goals. I see every day as a new day and a new opportunity.

> *"Knowing I am making a difference in the lives of children is what keeps me getting up each morning"*
>
> *— Jody Lintzenich*

Gwendolyn Paul

Blackwater FACE Program
Coolidge, Arizona

2002 Award Recipient

"I am very honored and grateful to know the teacher and the person Gwen Paul is. I know that she will have many more years of teaching and making learning fun. I hope that children in the future realize how very privileged and lucky they are to have a teacher like Gwen. Thank you again for all you have done."

— *Ellen Johns, Parent, Blackwater FACE Program*

My Habits to Share

- Reflect every day.
- Laugh with the children.
- Make everyone feel comfortable and welcome.

In 2002, when Gwendolyn Paul received her award for Toyota Teacher of the Year, she was in her 9th year of teaching preschool at the Blackwater Community School Family and Child Education (FACE) program—and in her 20th year of teaching overall. Today, in 2016, Gwen still teaches in the same preschool classroom at Blackwater and has wrapped up her 34th year of teaching.

After working with and teaching too many families and children to count, Gwen still possesses a strong dedication to the children and families of her Native American community.

> *Children are active learners who require concrete and relevant learning experiences that are essential for children in establishing a partnership of learning with their teachers, peer groups, and their families.*

The Blackwater FACE Program is part of the Blackwater Community School, located on the Gila River Indian Reservation, a 374,000-acre Indian Reservation in South Central Arizona. The Reservation is the fourth largest federally recognized Native American Tribe in the United States and consists of two distinct tribes the Pimas (Akimel O'Odham) and Maricopas (Pee Posh). The school serves families in several districts. The focus of the school is early childhood education and it serves children through fifth grade. The school was first operated as a Bureau of Indian Affairs (BIA) school in 1939, but in 1995 became a BIA grant school with a local school board.

Former Principal of Blackwater School, Jacqueline Powers shares that, "Gwen never wavered or lost the trust of families who enrolled in the FACE program. It is this legacy that has led to so many of the FACE families to stay with the program for several years, so that all of their children would benefit from Gwen as the extraordinary teacher they have come to love."

In the application for the Teacher of the Year award, Jacqueline discussed Gwen's commitment to families and their Native culture and language. "Gwen builds cultural components into her preschool curriculum so that the children learn about their Akimel O'Otham heritage. She teaches children the words of their kinship, home, and community. For many of these children, this may be their first exposure to their culture and language. In fact, the preservation of the O'Otham language has become a high priority because of the loss of this unique language. Currently, only a limited number of elders speak the language and at least two generations do not speak the language at all. Fortunately, Gwen is a fluent speaker and uses every opportunity in the FACE preschool to teach the children." Gwen has also worked with experts in the field of language and culture to create quality O'Otham children's books and curricula, based on the history of the tribe, the Gila River, and the O'Otham people.

Gwen established the Akimel O'Otham Basket Dancers to maintain the traditional dances of the culture and encouraged children as young as five years to join the group. The Basket Dancers have traveled all over the United States, Hong Kong, and New Zealand to share this cultural gift.

In addition to school and community involvement, Gwen served on state and national committees for developing state standards and was part of the committee to develop the Early Childhood/Preschool Standards for the Bureau of Indian Education.

Gwen shares, "Due to the longevity of the (FACE) program, we have gone through a lot, but we are positive. We always have the backing of the administrator and the school board. We deal with the changes and we're still here for the families. It's all about patience and having fun, and being there for the kids."

In Her Own Words

Gwen, you've worked with families for a long time. What is your greatest lesson learned?

I've learned that working with all these families, they all have the same issues, especially Native American families. They want their education for their child, and for themselves. Some find it harder to get started than others do. Families come in all sizes. We just need to be there for them and make sure they get what they need from the program. Make sure that they are comfortable, that they feel they can accomplish things.

In your years of education, if you could do anything over again, what would you do differently?

I think when I first started teaching preschool, I didn't really know how it would be in the early childhood field. I taught kindergarten before that, and it was a little different with Pre-K. My mindset was not set for three-and-four-year olds, but it didn't take me long to get to their level developmentally. Preschool takes a lot of patience.

What motivates you?

I think what motivates me is seeing the children come through that door, they are happy to be here. It takes some of them a long time to be ready to be happy. Some are really shy. It motivates me to keep them coming here every day, and seeing them happy. It's just who we are and how we are as Native Americans—we are all family. We make everyone feel comfortable and welcome, and that is important.

What advice do you want to share with other teachers who work with families?

Be open with parents. I think there always has to be that open communication with parents, whether the message is good or bad. They have to know we're here for them, because we are working with their children.

What kinds of things do you do on a daily basis that contribute to your teaching success?

At the end of every day, I try to sit back in a chair and reflect on the day. I talk with my paraprofessional and we discuss the day—how it went, what we would do differently, what needs to happen tomorrow.

I also think it is important to share something funny with the children every day and laugh. Laugh with the children. Kids can grow up knowing they can laugh, even if they are sad.

> "The longer a program exists, the more changes you will experience. The bottom line is that we deal with the changes, and we're still here for the families."
>
> *Gwen Paul — FACE Early Childhood Teacher, Blackwater Community School*

Cecilia Ramirez
Summit View Elementary
Pima Community College Family Literacy Program
Tucson, Arizona

——— 2001 Award Recipient ———

"Family literacy is more than a program, it's a value."

— Cecilia Ramirez

My Habits to Share

- Make a one-on-one connection with each student, every day. Even if it is only for a minute.
- Reflect. Self-evaluate. Daily.
- Be very thoughtful when working with families. Keep in mind their vast range of experiences.

"When I worked with Pima Adult Education, and I received this award, I felt it was our award, not mine. It was teamwork. After the award, I saw my role in a different way. I know that education is the foundation for a better life for the families and the children. For the community and for the country. But it was deeper for me.

"Family literacy is more than a program; it is a value. Even though I am retired, I carry that with me every day, to this day. This value is something we transfer to parents, and parents transfer to their children. Because the heart of family literacy is the parent and child working together, there is mutual learning for the future in order to accomplish goals.

"It's powerful. When we, the teachers, are able to teach a technique or strategy, we transfer the value to the parents, so they can internalize it, and then transfer that skill to their children. That keeps the program alive. Vibrant. It is more than a just program. It is change. It is the transformation.

"Receiving the award was a very special moment. I felt joy, but also responsibility and commitment to continue to carry this value forward. Every day. I'm so happy and grateful that I am a part of family literacy, to see the families grow, and to grow myself."

The center of all of this is the families. As long as
we keep that center strong, we continue.

In 2001, Cecilia Ramirez was the Adult Education teacher for the family literacy program at Pima Community College in Tucson, Arizona. She retired as the Advanced Program Coordinator there in 2014, but has carried her years of working in family literacy with her and continues to advocate for the program today.

The Pima Community College Family Literacy Program is a four-component family literacy program that supports parents as they work to get their GED, learn to speak better English, acquire job skills, and improve parenting skills. The adult education component was associated with Pima Adult and Family Literacy Corps (PAFLC), an AmeriCorps program. In the program, students gained valuable work skills, earned money for education, and developed an appreciation for the spirit of service through service learning projects.

At the time of the award, Cecilia had worked in the field of education for some 20 years and had taught in a family literacy program for six years as an adult education teacher in an elementary school-based program. She worked to help parents increase their education and to feel welcome and supported in the elementary school environment. She continually inspired her students to become leaders in the community. As the adult education instructor at Summit View Elementary School, she developed curriculum around her adult students' questions about children's education. By doing this, she was able to address topics that were relevant to both adults and children's educational needs.

At the time of her award, Principal Tony Covarrubia said, "Cecilia works extremely hard to make the parents feel they are a part of our school. She has assisted parents in getting involved in the PTO, literacy nights, math nights, and many other important activities. She is currently helping with the formation of a Summit View nature train and has encouraged parents to develop a community garden that they would attend to."

Cecilia worked with her students to discover their dreams and set goals they could work toward achieving. Parent Time activities were crucial to the success of the program. She used a team approach to ensure this success and worked to include the adult education team, school principal, and other staff members in assisting her.

Today, Cecilia talks of many lessons learned while working with families at Pima College. One prominent lesson centered on belief. She has always believed that you start with the student—that the student drives everything. She would tell her students: believe that you will succeed, believe that your child will go to college. One day, a student responded with, "It's not that we don't believe, it's that we don't have the tools and resources to make it happen."

After that, Cecilia began to look harder, more critically at what she was doing, and she began to provide more parent education and tools. She says, "That was a good conversation with the student, and it was a reminder for me that we always need to look at things from the student's perspective. Lack of basic services can be limiting. Look at the student, invest the time, and help them break their goals into smaller and smaller pieces so they are achievable." Cecilia adds, "We all have to respect each other's time and the commitments. I always strive for a respectful and safe environment. One where students can feel free to say, 'I don't want to do that.' I could find a way to still keep them engaged. Still teaching. Still learning. Honoring their interests while maintaining the integrity of the program. But it was their idea."

I am also a learner.

Cecilia believes in professional development. She also trained to be a certified trainer for the National Center for Family Literacy (now the National Center for Families Learning), where she could conduct professional development, as well. "The things I learned in professional development, I took back to my family literacy team, and also to the parents," she said. "We all worked as a whole. A comprehensive team. We learned that by working together, the benefit is so powerful for parents and the children."

In Her Own Words

Cecilia, you spent many years working with families. What motivated you day after day?

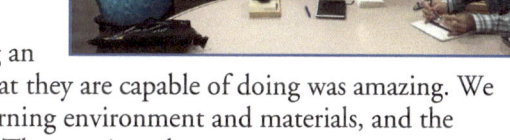

It's simple. Families hold the power within themselves—and just to be a part of providing an environment where parents could discover what they are capable of doing was amazing. We (the program) provided the respectful, safe learning environment and materials, and the parents took over. That was the amazing part. That motivated me.

What you are learning here is for your life. Just take it with you, and with that, all things can be possible.

Then there were the children—always so excited that their mommies were in the classroom with them. Learning with them. Watching this, and seeing the entire family transform—father, mother, and child—is also powerful.

Paying it forward. What are some of your best teaching practices you would you like to share with other teachers?

There are many, but here are a few.

Have roles for your students. Have committees in your classroom—committees that impact the program, like students who are liaisons with school administrative staff, technology and social committees, program presentations, and so on. Whatever roles make sense for your classroom. The goal is for all of the adult students to have a role, and when you do that, it gives birth to a lot of things. These committees go beyond the classroom, to the greater school, and also to work with community. Rotate roles and responsibilities, perhaps quarterly.

Form a literacy council. The adult students and parents created the council and did various things in the school and community. They spoke at events and school board meetings. They became the voice of the program. This can be shaped in many ways. The literacy council often attended meetings at the library and in the community, together as a group. It was powerful to see so many parents interested and engaged.

Make a personal connection each morning. I did this every day, and it was very powerful. In the mornings, I would ask, "How many are here in class today? Who is absent?" We would verbalize who was there, who wasn't. Then, for those who were not there, I'd ask, "Have you heard anything about this person today?" The point was concern and caring, and for them to develop a deeper understanding of the value of school attendance. Part of our family was missing. I'd say to the class, "Does this person need support and how can we support her?" Or, to the social committee, "Should we get a card?" This caring and support for each other every morning helped build our community of learners.

Institute a buddy system. Each person had another person to work with. If anyone missed a day of school, the other person communicated to the buddy what they missed that day. The buddy was responsible for catching them up.

Cecilia, when you were teaching, were there things you did habitually that you felt better equipped you for working with families?

Yes. I always tried to make a one-on-one connection with each student every day, even if it is only for a minute. My students knew I would stay after class and make myself available. Parents knew I was there with them.

I also reflected a lot. A self-evaluation. I would think about what happened today, what was the goal, what was the outcome? And then I would transfer that to the next learning. Journal writing was an important part of our class. The students wrote in their journals once or twice a week. When they wrote, I wrote. I always kept my own journal. I was always reflecting on my teaching.

Be very thoughtful every day in knowing that we are working with families who have a range of experiences and backgrounds. Keep that in mind. These are great people.

It is an honor, and a privilege, to work with families.

— *Cecilia Ramirez*

Sharonrose McMarr-Schroeder

San Pedro/Narbonne Adult School
Los Angeles, California

2000 Award Recipient

"In Sharon I have found an excellent teacher and friend."

— *Olga Hinojos, Student*

Sharonrose McMarr-Schroeder was an adult education/ESL teacher of the San Pedro/Norbonne Community Adult School in Los Angeles in the year 2000, when she was chosen for the Teacher of the Year honor. Ms. McMarr-Schroeder was chosen as a part of the celebration of the National Family Literacy Day. She was a six-year teacher and created a number of special family literacy program designs that she wove into the existing curriculum. Those projects emphasized language, teamwork, communication, and motivation to learn. These were especially helpful to her English as a Second Language (ESL) parents. She also developed a multi-media network center at the school, which gave the parents a new dimension for learning. The center offered students the opportunity to become technologically experienced, introducing them to the world of computers, e-mail, voice mail, and problem solving through directed teaching and computerized learning. She and her student parents were involved in many community activities with several local foundations.

Olga Hinojos, a family literacy parent said, "In Sharon I have found an excellent teacher and friend. Because of her tenacity and continuous encouragement, I progressed quickly and my self-esteem improved. She knew how to motivate everyone in the class to learn."

Dayle Bailey

Richmond County Even Start
Rockingham, North Carolina

1999 Award Recipient

"By knowing and learning from Mrs. Bailey, I found that my dreams became a reality. I am a better parent and provider for my children. She has inspired me and given me confidence in myself. Because of Mrs. Bailey, I am now a college student, something I believed could not happen for me."

— Kelly Tuttle, Student

My Habits to Share

- Read, and pass on the love of reading.
- Find solutions to make things better.
- Find the humor in everyday life.

Finding herself living in a new part of the country—after moving from California to North Carolina—with different dialects, customs, and even culture, Dayle Bailey felt like she'd been transplanted to another planet. She wanted to go home, but she knew that was impossible. So, she dug in, adjusted to her new lifestyle, signed up for college classes, and concentrated on finding the good in her life.

Years later, degree in hand, Dayle started working with adult students and realized that they, too, likely felt transplanted to another planet when they took that difficult step to go back to school and stepped into her classroom.

The big lesson that I have learned is not to wish for what you can't have, but to make the best of what you do have.

Dayle Baily, Adult and Parenting Educator at the Richmond County Even Start Family Literacy Project, was chosen for the 1999 Teacher of the Year award as part of the National Family Literacy Day celebration. She had taught for five years at Rohanen Primary School where she encouraged the strengths of her students and helped them to discover their own abilities.

During her tenure, absenteeism was replaced by participation. Parents became actively involved in the PTO, attended parent/teacher conferences, and began to further their education and secure jobs. At the same time, a strong bond between parents and staff was formed.

The Richmond County Even Start Project based at Rohanen Primary School was located in the most economically depressed area of the county. The school was the center of activity in the community, but before the Even Start family literacy project was implemented, it had met with thwarted efforts to motivate any substantial level of parent involvement. Little value seemed to be placed on learning, the school, or the parents' role in their children's education. Through Even Start and Dayle's adult class, things began to change. A bond between school staff and parents developed as a result of parents' participation in family literacy. These adults became the school's strongest supporters. Dayle's students gained confidence in their abilities to learn and lead, and became spokespersons for the school and family literacy.

According to Ann McNeely, program coordinator, "The knowledge, skills, and talents of Dayle Bailey were a major contributing factor in the success of the family literacy program. The outcome data from the adult/parenting education components spoke to her ability to motivate adult students in setting and meeting higher expectations for themselves and their children." Dayle created learning environments where adults felt welcome and valued, regardless of their needs, circumstances, or attitudes.

Dayle understood the importance of extended opportunities for parents and children to learn and interact together around books and other learning activities. For example, when the preschool children were learning about windy weather, the adult students used reading and math skills to create kites for their preschoolers. The children joined their parents in decorating the kites and together, they enjoyed flying them. As they explored the characteristics of wind, parents and children had an opportunity to practice problem solving.

I love it when reading becomes a fun, interactive, intergenerational event.

Today, Dayle is retired, and has three grown children, five grandchildren (ages 3-18 years), three step grandchildren, and two step great-grandchildren. Between work and attending kids' birthday parties, she says she stays quite busy!

Dayle shares the following: "Once my children were in school, I returned to college and graduated from UNC Pembroke, at age 32, with a BA in English Education. I taught four years at Richmond Senior High School and then was hired to teach in the Even Start Family Literacy Program. Along with then Even Start Coordinator Ann McNeely, I helped establish the Adult Education/Parenting Component and worked in the program for eight years. Then I returned to UNC Pembroke and earned a Master's Degree in English Education. For the next eight years, I taught Freshman Composition at UNCP and at Richmond Community College in Hamlet, NC. I am now retired from teaching and am co-owner, with my husband, of Delco, Inc., a trucking company that he ran alone until I retired. I miss teaching and would consider returning to part time teaching once I retire from our business."

In Her Own Words

Dayle, what are some lessons learned you could share with us about working with families?

The socio-economic status of a family is not necessarily a predictor of how the children in that family will fare. What is important to their future is that children are reared by a parent or parents, regardless of race, gender, or religion, who establish a home that is loving, nurturing, and safe for their children.

How do you pay it forward?

One thing that I am committed to is that all children, beginning at an early age, should be exposed to, and/or part of, live entertainment and cultural events. This could be a school play, a community theater, a concert in the park, or a large event. After witnessing my little grandkids' excitement when we took them to a Little Mermaid's ballet, I began to donate money to help school children, who otherwise could not afford it, to attend live events at Blumenthal Performing Arts Center in Charlotte, NC. Through our company, my husband and I also donated a sizeable amount to help establish a Discovery Place Kids in our small town, which has been a great asset to our community.

Can you share three habits of yours you think other teachers may benefit from knowing?

I love, love, love to read, and I try to pass along this love of reading to my family, my friends, and the families I worked with. One of my favorite memories is reading "Stone Soup" during parenting. The parents then put on a Stone Soup play, complete with costumes, for the preschool children. After the play, the children got to eat Stone Soup with their parents. This was one of many collaborative experiences between our preschoolers and their parents and all the staff and families had a great time. I love it when reading becomes a fun, interactive, intergenerational event.

Rather than dwell on how things should be, I try to find solutions to make things better. I try to avoid the "I Wish" or the "If Only" habit. I read somewhere that what happens to us is not as important as our attitude toward it. My adult students had challenging, often dissatisfying lives, and together we worked on finding positive solutions for problems.

I love to find the humor in everyday life and try to avoid negative people and situations. I feel that I carried this attitude into my teaching and interactions with parents, children, and other staff members.

> *"The level and quality of parent participation in a family literacy project is the key to program success and ultimately to positive changes in family attitudes, behaviors, and resources. Building on this premise, Dayle Bailey uses all resources available to her to motivate the adult students in taking full advantage of the services family literacy has to offer."*
>
> — *Ann McNeely, Program Coordinator*

1999

Anita Koch
Glades Tri-City Even Start
Belle Glade, Florida

———— **1998 Award Recipient** ————

At the time of her award, Anita Koch had been an educator for over 35 years and coordinator and adult education instructor for the Glades Tri-City Family Education Program in Belle Glade, Florida, since 1993. Her experience included teaching fifth grade, pre- and basic adult literacy, ESOL classes, and adult education/GED classes. She was also a dance/fitness instructor and nutrition/cooking instructor.

It was reported that Anita drove over 100 miles each day to and from her two-room country schoolhouse. At the time of this award, she had logged in 72,000 miles, the equivalent of 12 round trips across America or 2.5 trips around the world. She made this trip from the urban coast of Palm Beach County through almost 50 miles of sugar cane and vegetable crops to the isolated town of Belle Glade, because she truly enjoyed her students and the family literacy program she worked so hard to develop. One of the keys to Anita's success was that she was very flexible, setting the classroom schedule to meet the students' work schedules in the fields. She also helped them in every aspect of their lives, from finding mentors to assisting them with welfare reform needs.

But most importantly, Anita made certain that her students knew they were valuable participants and valued members of the Tri-City family. Her approach worked. Over three years, eight students obtained their GEDs, five students obtained U.S. citizenship, 18 secured employment in such jobs as security guards, child care work, clerical work, and one parent enrolled in a four-year college. Several parents went on to vocational training. Anita's on-going concern for her parents made a difference in their lives and in the lives of their families.

Karen Klima-Thomas
Family Tree Project
Lowell Elementary School, Mesa, Arizona

--- **1997 Award Recipient** ---

"Karen encourages the children and supports them in whatever they try to do. She always sends the message that 'You can do it."

— *Parent, Mesa Family Tree Project*

My Habits to Share

- Be kind.
- No judging.
- Read, read, read.

According to Karen Klima-Thomas, "Family literacy is about planting seeds. You really never know if the seeds will take root and grow. Years later, you may experience unexpected, heart-warming encounters that give evidence of that seed growing into a beautiful and strong tree. Or maybe not. Your job remains the same—plant the seeds."

In 1990, Karen was the first preschool teacher at the Family Tree Project's original site, Lowell Elementary School, an Even Start family literacy program in Mesa, Arizona. As a member of the program development team, Karen played a significant role in establishing the high standards of quality that have guided the Mesa program throughout the years.

Karen identifies with this philosophy of Fred Rogers. "If only you could sense how important you are to the lives of those you meet; how important you can be to people you may never even dream of. There is something of yourself you leave at every meeting with another person."

> *Being able to experience the children's wide-eyed wonder at what I was showing them of the world was an every-day delight for me.*

According to the program director, Marilyn Box, "Karen was an exceptional early childhood educator with a solid understanding of child development and who effectively supported children's learning and development by creating opportunities in the classroom that reflected her students' needs and interests. She had a remarkable ability to help parents recognize their role as their children's first teachers, and to support them in expanding their knowledge and skills. Karen served as a mentor to other family literacy educators, taking on a variety of leadership and training roles within the school district and the state."

> *My team was everything—my own team at my school and the Family Tree Project in total. We were so lucky to come together. I was so lucky to be a part of something that changed so many lives.*

When asked about receiving her award, Karen said, "When I accepted the award at the convention, I stated that I would not be up there were it not for Marilyn Box and the whole Family Tree team. I believe that to this day. Linda Mead [adult education teacher] and I clicked from the very first time we met. She was the best teacher partner I could have ever had. We had many adventures together, especially during home visits. My aide, Sally Galvan, was invaluable to me. She was the only one I interviewed for the job because I knew she was perfect. She helped me with my 'sink or swim' Spanish. I once told an inconsolable little girl (in Spanish) that her mother would be back 'in a little mouse!' The little girl looked at me, very surprised. Sally corrected my Spanish to 'in a little while.' She did stop crying, though! Both Sally and Linda are dear friends to this day."

When Karen retired in 2005, the local district employee newsletter said the following: "The impact of her high expectations is measured through the growth of the children and their parents. They thrive under her guidance with language skills, child development, confidence, and spending time together one-on-one. Karen has been a mentor and trainer in the Mesa Family Tree Project and in family literacy programs throughout Arizona and the United States. She is a pioneer, an inspiration. Karen's colleagues are grateful for her hard work and dedication that have paved the way for those who follow."

Today, Karen still believes in planting those seeds and leaving something of yourself behind for others. Retired now, she's still planting seeds, although in different ways. She does volunteer work—reading to folks losing their eyesight and serving as a beta reader for a British author. Her roots, however, are still firmly planted in family literacy.

In Her Own Words

What are some lessons learned from your family literacy experience?

All families love their children dearly and want only the best for them. They may be unsure about how to encourage and support their children. It is the role of family literacy to show them how to do this. Family literacy educators are teachers and students, giving support to and learning from the families. That is the strength of the family literacy model. This quote from Jeanette Rankin speaks to me as well: "You take people as far as they will go, not as far as you would like them to go."

We did realize early on that we would need to present parenting information in Spanish and we hadn't anticipated that. In lieu of that, perhaps be sure to know your target group before beginning the family literacy adventure. In truth, I enjoyed every minute of my career as a family literacy educator. I look back on my years in The Family Tree Project with a great deal of pride and love.

What motivated your work with families, day in and day out?

I always knew I would be a teacher, even when I was young. The college I attended only trained teachers at the onset of my years there. I am and have always been a people person. Working with the mothers was a joyful learning experience for me. Going on home visits and being welcomed into families' homes was touching and so insightful. Being able to experience the children's wide-eyed wonder at what I was showing them of the world was an everyday delight for me. Seeing changes in both the mothers and in the children, and in the mothers and the children working together, was so inspirational. Every day was a new adventure.

Can you identify a few habits of yours that you feel contributed to your success?

Every day, I work to live up to this quote by Henry James: "Three things in human life are important: The first is to be kind. The second is to be kind. And the third is to be kind."

No judging! I don't know enough to judge anyone about anything!

I read, read, read. I have always read, read, read. Giving books to children, to parents with new babies, is one of my life's delights! There is nothing that will serve a child better than growing a joy of reading.

> "[Karen] is a pioneer, an inspiration. Karen's colleagues are grateful for her hard work and dedication that have paved the way for those who follow."
>
> — *MesAgenda*, May 11, 2005

Section Three

INTRODUCTION TO SECTION 3

Section 3 provides a snapshot of information about each *Toyota Family Teacher of the Year* recipient and his or her school, including:

- The award year from 1997 to 2016
- The teacher's name and title at the time of the award
- The name of the program or school that received the award, with updated information if the school/program name has changed since the time of the award.
- Contact information:
  - For the teacher, if the teacher agreed
  - For the school or program. We have listed the varying types of contact information provided to us.
- The teacher's biography—as provided to us.
- A listing of the runners-up for the award for that particular year.

PROGRAM INFORMATION AND TEACHER BIOGRAPHIES

Award Year – 1997

Karen Klima-Thomas

Early Childhood Teacher, Lowell Elementary School

Mesa Family Tree Project, Mesa Public Schools

Mesa, Arizona

Contact Information: karenkt17@cox.net

Bio: I grew up in a small suburb of Chicago. I attended a one school district—grades K-8. I returned to teach there when I earned my teaching degree. Some of my teachers were still there! Teaching Sunday school when I was in high school cemented my decision to be a teacher. I graduated from Illinois State University. in 1965. I married my college sweetheart. I taught middle grades for three years and left teaching to raise our three children. As a "full-time mom," I tutored a bit and had small preschool classes in our home. Moving to Tucson and then to Mesa, I returned to teaching in 1983—Kindergarten and Pre-K. I acquired a M.Ed. Degree with an early childhood education emphasis from Arizona State University. I met Marilyn Box who was starting a family literacy program in Mesa Public Schools. I became the first preschool teacher. Our team was a well-oiled machine. As the program grew, I added facilitation of trainings and workshops to my résumé, which I enjoyed almost as much as being in the classroom. I retired in May of 2005. After retiring, I consulted in both family literacy and preschool programs. I am now fully retired but have been known to pass out books to children and to deliver parenting advice in the grocery store!

Runners-up: N/A

Award Year – 1998

Anita Koch

Coordinator/Adult Education, Glades Tri-City Even Start Family Literacy Project

Belle Glade, Florida

Contact Information: N/A

Bio: At the time of the award, Anita Koch had been an educator for over 35 years and coordinator and adult instructor for the Glades Tri-City Family Education Program in Belle Glade, Florida, since 1993. Her experience included teaching fifth grade, pre- and basic adult literacy, ESOL classes, and adult education/GED classes. She was also a dance/fitness instructor and nutrition/cooking instructor.

Runners-up: Jacquelyn Power, Blackwater, Arizona; Sara Bramer, St. Louis, MO; Jeanette F. Lawson, Coushatta, Louisiana; Roxie Oberg, Binghampton, New York

Award Year – 1999

Dayle Bailey

Adult Education Teacher, Richmond County Even Start Family Literacy Program

Rockingham County, North Carolina

Contact Information: dayle.bailey@yahoo.com

Bio: Once my children were in school, I returned to college and graduated from UNC Pembroke, at age 32, with a B.A. in English Education. I taught four years at Richmond Senior High School and then was hired to teach in the Even Start Family Literacy Program. Along with then Even Start Coordinator Ann McNeely, I helped establish the Adult Education/Parenting Component and worked in the program for eight years. Then I returned to UNC Pembroke and earned a Master's Degree in English Education. For the next eight years, I taught Freshman Composition at UNCP and at Richmond Community College in Hamlet, NC. I am now retired from teaching and am co-owner, with my husband, of Delco, Inc., a trucking company that he ran alone until I retired. I miss teaching, however, and am planning on returning to part time teaching at Richmond Community College next semester. I have three grown children, five grandchildren (ages 3-18 years), three step grandchildren, and two step great-grandchildren. Between work and attending kids' birthday parties, I stay quite busy!

Runners-up: Jeanette Lawson, Coushatta, Louisiana; Karna Mikkelson, Bloomington, MN; Karol Machmeier, Eau Claire, Wisconsin; Beth Yokom, New Brighton, MN

Award Year – 2000

Sharonrose McMarr-Schroeder

Adult Education/ESL Teacher, San Pedro/Narbonne Community Adult School

Los Angeles, California

Contact Information: N/A

Bio: Sharonrose McMarr-Schroeder was an adult education/ESL teacher with the San Pedro/Narbonne Community Adult School in Los Angeles. Mrs. McMarr-Schroeder was chosen as a part of the celebration of National Family Literacy Day. She was a six-year teacher and created a number of special family literacy program designs that she wove into the existing curriculum. These projects emphasized language, teamwork, communication, and motivation to learn. She also developed a multi-media network center at the school, which gave the parents a new dimension for learning.

Runners-up: Gloria Williams, Tucson, Arizona; Ann Chandler, Monroe, Louisiana

Award Year – 2001

Cecilia Ramirez

Adult Education Teacher/Supervisor, Summit View Elementary and Pima Community College Tucson, Arizona

Contact Information:

Pima Community College, Adult Basic Education for College and Career

Phone: 520-206-3987 | Email: adulted@pima.edu

Bio: In 2001, Cecilia Ramirez was the adult education teacher for the family literacy program at Pima Community College in Tucson, Arizona. She retired as the advanced program coordinator there in 2014, but has carried her years of working in family literacy with her, and continues to advocate for the program today. Cecelia had worked in the field of education for some 20 years and had taught a family literacy program for six years as an adult education teacher in an elementary school-based program. As the adult education instructor at Summit View Elementary School, she developed curriculum around her adult students' questions about their children's education. Ms. Ramirez also became a certified trainer for the National Center for Family Literacy and trained other teachers in family literacy professional development.

Runners-up: Sandy Cunningham, Hopkinsville, Kentucky; Beatriz Diaz, Miami, Florida; Sarah Hornback, Hodgenville, Kentucky

---

Award Year – 2002

Gwendolyn Paul

Early Childhood Teacher, Blackwater Community School FACE program

Coolidge, Arizona

Contact Information: N/A

Bio: In 2002, when Gwendolyn Paul received her award for Toyota Teacher of the Year, she was in her 9th year of teaching preschool at the Blackwater Community School FACE program—and in her 20th year of teaching overall. Today, in 2016, Gwen still teaches in the same preschool classroom at Blackwater and has wrapped up her 34th year of teaching. The Family and Child Education (FACE) program at Blackwater Community School provides for the unique educational and cultural needs of American Indian families. A member of the Pima tribe, Ms. Paul worked in education in her community for some 23 years (at the time of the award) with eight years of service in family literacy programs. A major goal of Ms. Paul's was to preserve the language and culture of the Akimel O'odham people. She is a fluent speaker of the language.

Runners-up: Judith Moffitt, Barberton, Ohio; Julia Wagner, Marrero, Louisiana; Beverly Woliver, Parkers Lake, Kentucky

Award Year – 2003

Jody Lintzenich

Elementary Teacher/ESL Instructor, Haywood Elementary, Nashville Public Schools

Nashville, Tennessee

Contact Information: jodylintzenich@hotmail.com

Bio: After attending Limestone Grade School and Herscher High School, I spent a year as a secretary before deciding to attend Illinois State University and major in elementary education. I felt I had a rapport with children, as I had taken care of my younger siblings, had spent many hours babysitting, and spent time working with children at my church. After graduating from Illinois State University in 1977, my first job was teaching first, second, and third grade all in one classroom. I did that for three years before transferring to Herscher Grade School to teach first grade for five years. I moved to Nashville in 1986 and taught second grade for three years at Berry Elementary, then transferred to Haywood Elementary. During this time I went back to college with a fellow teacher and earned a Master's Degree in Administration/Supervision and an Education Specialist Degree in Curriculum and Instruction. Four years later I attended Carson Newman College and earned a Master's Degree in Teaching English as a Second Language. I then became involved in the Toyota Families in Schools program. In the fall of 2003, I transferred to Whitsitt Elementary and taught there until I retired in 2015. Currently I teach small groups of reading or math at Maxwell Elementary. What a joy to see the progress children can make with more individualized instruction.

Runners-up: Martha Crowe, Fremont, California; Marlene Porter, Florence, South Carolina; Cathy Shoulders, Roanoke, Virginia

---

Award Year – 2004

Lorie Preheim

Adult Education/ESL Instructor, Briya Public Charter School

Washington, DC

Contact Information: Lorie Preheim

2333 Ontario Road NW, Washington, DC 20009 | 202-232-7777
http://briya.org/ | https://www.facebook.com/BriyaPCS/ | https://twitter.com/briyapcs

Bio: Lorie Preheim is Briya Public Charter School's academic dean and charter school founder. She has been with the school for 18 years and has 24 years of experience in the field of adult education and family literacy. Ms. Preheim earned a Master's Degree in Adult Education from George Mason University and a B.A. in Education, International Development, and Art from Bethel College. She was named Toyota Teacher of the Year (2004) by Toyota and the National Center for Family Literacy and sits on the Adult Education Performance Management Framework task force for the Public Charter School Board. She has been board president for the Learning Disabilities Association, DC Chapter, and has continued to volunteer for the organization since 2005.

Runners-up: Shari M. Brown, Lenoir, North Carolina; Amy Hall, Wilson, Michigan; Alice Levine, Boston, Massachusetts; Anne M. Morgan, St. Petersburg, Florida

Award Year - 2005

Amy Hall

Early Childhood Teacher, Hannahville Community School FACE program

Wilson, Michigan

Contact Information: amy.hall@hannahvilleschool.net

Hannahville FACE Program, Wilson, Michigan | 906-723-2711

Bio: Amy Hall holds a Bachelor's Degree with teacher certification in Child Care, Family Life Education, and Home Economics. Prior to her work with FACE, Amy was the coordinator of the local Early On program, which provided early intervention services to the local Indian community. She was the early childhood teacher for the Hannahville Family and Child Education (FACE) program on the Potowatomi Reservation, Hannahville, Michigan, at the time of her award. She has extensive experience working with children from birth to five years of age, in her community and in northern Michigan. Eleven years after the Teacher of the Year honor, and after 18 years of working in the Hannahville FACE program, Amy is still very much involved in working with families. A few years ago, she traded her preschool teacher hat to work more closely with the adults in the adult education classroom.

Runners-up: Vanda Guffey, Albany, Kentucky; Melcenia Sprowls-Shelton, Hodgenville, Kentucky; Susan Taylor, Eldorado Springs, Colorado

---

Award Year - 2006

Mark Faloni

Adult Education/ESL Instructor, Briya Public Charter School

Washington, DC

Contact Information: mfaloni@briya.org

2333 Ontario Road NW, Washington, DC 20009 | 202-232-7777
http://briya.org/ | https://www.facebook.com/BriyaPCS/ | https://twitter.com/briyapcs

Bio: After graduating from college with degrees in Spanish and education, I knew I wanted to work in the Latino community in some aspect. I am originally from Baltimore and there wasn't a huge Latino community in Baltimore in the late 1980's, so I decided to move closer to DC, where the immigrant population was much larger. My professional career began when I took a job with an Even Start Program, which had a one-year grant working with Latino high schoolers and their babies, so the mothers could continue their high school education. That was 1990 and Rebecca Roberts, the director who wrote the grant, hired me to be the ESL teacher. It was basically the two of us and two part-time people, banging on apartment doors asking residents if they knew of any immigrants, who wanted to learn English for free, while we taught their small children at the same time. That was difficult, but going pretty well and we found a handful of participants. Well, Rebecca left after about two years and left me as the director. I went to four huge meetings with DC bigwigs, who pushed a lot of paper around, dressed to the nines, talked a big game and did nothing that they proposed to do. I knew this wasn't for me and that I wanted to be with the people in the classroom teaching and learning, so I had to find another director. I found Christie McKay (I hired my own boss!) and we have been at it for the past 20-some years, growing the program into what it is today. Currently, we are in three, soon to be four buildings, including the one we just purchased. We have upwards of 450-500 student families on a yearly basis and have connected and collaborated with Mary's Center, a huge multicultural, low income clinic in DC. Our plan and vision is that educated families can be healthier families, understanding their rights and advocating for themselves and their loved ones. We now have roughly 75 workers just in the Briya PCS educational section of the program alone.

Runners-up: Jason Tetrault, Providence, Rhode Island; John Fullen, Coolidge, Arizona; Kay Brown, Monroe, Louisiana

---

Award Year – 2007

Gretchen White Conway

Coordinator/Early Childhood Teacher, Caldwell County Schools

Caldwell County, North Carolina

Contact Information: kssnowhite@charter.net

Bio: Gretchen White Conway earned her B.A. in Elementary Education and Theatre Arts with a minor in English and Music from Kansas Wesleyan University and an M.Ed. in Educational Psychology/Early Childhood Special Education from Wichita State University. Her teaching career started in 1981 in Wichita, Kansas, where she fell in love with working with young children with disabilities and their families. Gretchen worked for early childhood programs in Kansas and in Arizona on the Colorado River Indian Tribe Reservation with children from four Indian tribes and migrant Mexican families. On the reservation, she was also a CDA instructor to teachers and parents, who became teacher assistants. In Kansas, she was a practicum coordinator and instructor for pre-special education teachers at a college consortium, Associated Colleges of Central Kansas (ACCK), and co-developed a curriculum, Navigating the Resource Maze. In North Carolina, she served as the early childhood coordinator for the Caldwell County Even Start Family Literacy program, where in March of 2007, she was selected to be the Toyota Family Literacy Teacher of the Year. She has presented at CEC/DEC International Conference, the 2006 National Conference on Family Literacy, and various state conferences. As a children's advocate, she also served on the NC Infant/Toddler Guidelines Committee. After leaving family literacy, she remains with the Caldwell County Schools as a preschool teacher and participates in long-range planning for the preschool within the school district. Gretchen enjoys facilitating children's learning, supporting parent's goals and being a part of a large family of learners.

Runners-up: Mary Beth Morgan, Watertown, Maine; John Fullen, Coolidge, Arizona; Andrea Stridiron, Rochester, New York

Award Year – 2008

Katy Kibbey

Adult Education/ESL Instructor, Wayne Metro Family Literacy

Hamtramck, Michigan

Contact Information: kkibbey@waynemetro.org
Katy Kibbey | Chief Programs Officer
Wayne Metro Community Action Agency | 7310 Woodward, Suite 800
Detroit, Michigan 48202 | Wayne Metro website: www.waynemetro.org

Bio: In 2012, I was promoted from my position as family literacy director to chief programs officer for the agency. I am currently responsible for overseeing all agency program departments that support our agency's mission of empowering low-income individuals and strengthening communities through diverse services that address the causes and conditions of poverty. My current duties include program implementation and day-to-day operations, annual and department budgets, grant compliance, information management, and outcome monitoring, and I serve as part of the senior administration team reporting to the CEO.

Runners-up: Misti Lauer, Sterling, Colorado; Milene Panzica, Shelby County, Alabama; Silvana Vasconcelos, New York, New York

---

Award Year – 2009

María Antonia Piñón

Early Childhood Teacher, Riverside Elementary School, All-Aboard Family Literacy Program, Miami, Florida

Contact Information: mav3548@gmail.com

Cell: 305 761-6640 | All-Aboard Family Literacy Program
Institute for Child and Family Health, Inc. | 15490 NW 7th Avenue, Suite 204
Miami, Florida 33169 | 305 685-2227 | Website: icfhinc.org

Bio: Maria Pinon worked in the All-Aboard Family Literacy Program at Riverside Elementary School in the Dade County Schools. Armed with 20 years of education experience, she turned her focus to family literacy. She built and expanded the program with the belief in the power of families and the importance of children entering school with the skills they needed to succeed. Her impact saw measurable achievements for families and she had a positive, contagious attitude that sparked community involvement and interest in her program. Originally a teacher and school counselor, Maria learned about a program called Even Start in the late 80s and early 90s, and eventually the school district where she worked acquired an Even Start program. She saw the changes in families and applied for the coordinator position. Over the years, Maria worked in the program, and then moved overseas for a while to work in an orphanage. When she moved back to the states, she began working in Miami for the All-Aboard program. Today, Maria has been retired for four years and lives in Texas, where she spends time with her family and helps take care of grandchildren.

Runners-up: Susan Seay, Shelby County, Alabama; Arturo Muro, El Pason, Texas; Karen Hertzier, Washington, DC

Award Year – 2010

Karen Kay Brown

Adult Education/ESL Instructor/Coordinator, Union Parish Family Literacy

Bernice, Louisiana

Contact Information: kbrown@ladelta.edu

Union Parish Family Literacy and Adult Educational Center, Bernice, Louisiana
Cell: 318-368-5075 | Office: 318-28509857

Bio: Karen "Kay" Brown has stated she cannot imagine doing anything except teaching family literacy and adult education. Kay has a Louisiana teaching certificate in elementary and adult education, and over 30 years of experience teaching children, adults, and families of Union Parish, Louisiana. In 2010 she was named the Toyota Family Literacy Teacher of the Year by the National Center for Family Literacy. She was also awarded the National Outstanding Teacher of the Year Award in 2013 by the Commission on Adult Basic Education. While Kay Brown is proud to be a wife, mother of two, grandmother of four, church member, and family member to many in her local area, her community identity is most strongly linked to her work. She carries her passion for adult education and family literacy everywhere she goes, promoting the DeltaLINC Union Parish Adult and Family Literacy Center to elected officials, business owners, news media, and friends, Kay refuses to stand alone in the limelight for the program's accomplishments, giving credit to her coworkers for their successes. She views adults/parents as the change agent in the family and as a child's first and most important teacher, and believes we are limited only by own motivation and imagination.

Runners-up: Rosa Hernandez, Long Beach, California; Norma Sandoval-Shinn, Tuscon, Arizona; Gayle Von Keyserling, Palmyra, Virgina

---

Award Year – 2011

Patricia Urdialez

Adult Education Teacher, Mesa Public Schools

Mesa, Arizona

Contact Information: pjurdialez@mpsaz.org

Bio: My name is Patricia J. Arzt (Urdialez) I received my B.S. in Business degree from New Mexico State University in 1986. I worked in the business field a few years, but my education experience began as a volunteer in my son's classroom. I moved into my career path of adult education, my passion, in 2004. I am currently teaching English Language Acquisition for Adults and Family Literacy at Mesa Public Schools. In addition, I am the college and career readiness coordinator for Mesa Public Schools Community Education Department. I am a strong advocate for empowering adult students with life and language skills. I involve my students in real-life activities and conversations in the classroom and encourage them to actively participate in their community and their children's education. I am a member of the board for the Mesa Association of Hispanic Citizens as well as a member of the Arizona Association of Lifelong Learners. Above all, I believe that education should be fun and help students make a positive contribution to our world.

Runners-up: Shari Brown, Lenoir, North Carolina; Lisa Lokesak, Union, Kentucky; Cheryl R. Williams, Norfolk, Virginia

Award Year – 2012

Shari Brown

Adult Education Teacher/Coordinator, Caldwell County, North Carolina

Contact Information: sbrown@cccti.edu

Bio: Shari Brown, director of the Adult Education and Family Literacy Program in Lenoir, North Carolina, has been employed by Caldwell Community College for 22 years. She holds a B.S. in Child Development and Family Relations with a K-6 Certification from the University of North Carolina at Greensboro. Her M.A. is in Higher Education, Developmental Studies with a concentration in Counseling from Appalachian State University. Shari was awarded the 2011 Great Teacher Award for Caldwell Community College and the Toyota National Family Literacy Teacher of the Year in 2012. She has also been the recipient of the Respecting Diversity Leadership Award from the Caldwell County Schools. Currently, Shari serves on the Board of Directors for Blue Ridge Community Action and the North Carolina Pre-K committee. Her certifications include, but are not limited to: Manager in Program Improvement, Basic Skills Resource Specialist, Multisensory Language Instruction, Motheread, and Working Smart. Shari's training as a Payne Learning Needs Screener and Irlen Screener assist her in supporting individual learning styles. She enjoys sharing ideas with presentations at national and state conferences. Her presentations include, but are not limited to: The Power of Teaching through Projects, Intergenerational Writing, and Teamwork: Building strong ties within your program. She is an advocate of cultural awareness and diversity. Bringing families with different values and beliefs together provides a wonderful learning environment for her students. Shari loves to explore and engage in outdoor activities such as bicycling, hiking, kayaking, and camping with her family.

Runner-up: Karen Routt, Indianapolis, Indiana

Award Year – 2013

Carolyn Blocker

Adult Education Teacher, Long Beach Unified School District Family Literacy

Long Beach, California

Contact Information: N/A

Bio: I am still doing my favorite job, which is being the mom to three great kids, Thomas (20), William (17), and Anna (13). I am also fortunate to be the children's ministry director at my church. This is my 28th year in education. After spending the last 10 years working with families, I am returning to the elementary classroom this fall. The skills I have learned while being a part of the family literacy program will benefit me as I take on this new, old experience.

Runner-up: Mary Ellen Lesniak

Award Year – 2014

Elizabeth Atack

Library Program Manager, Nashville Public Library

Nashville, Tennessee

Contact Information: Elizabeth.Atack@nashville.gov

Nashville Public Library, 615 Church Street, Nashville, TN 37219

Phone: 615-862-5773 | Web: http://www.library.nashville.org

We're on Facebook as Nashville Public Library, and on Instagram and Twitter as @nowatnpl

Bio: Elizabeth (Liz) Atack works at Nashville Public Library (NPL), where she oversees Bringing Books to Life (BBTL), a preschool literacy outreach program. In addition to managing the program's daily and long range operations, she is on the front lines of helping kids learn (and love!) to read, juggling story times, trainings for teachers and reading workshops for parents. Under her leadership, BBTL has won local and national awards and, in 2014, she was named the *Toyota Family Teacher of the Year* by the National Center for Families Learning. Locally, Liz is the vice chair of Alignment Nashville's Pre-K Team and serves on advisory boards for local early education and parent engagement organizations. Before coming to NPL in 2007, Liz was a teacher and museum educator. She graduated from Oberlin College in Oberlin, Ohio, and holds a Master's Degree in Childhood Museum Education from Bank Street College of Education in New York City.

Runners-up: Kathleen Johnson, Phoenix, Arizona

Award Year – 2015

Kristen Whitaker

High School History Teacher, Columbia Heights Educational Campus

Washington, DC

Contact Information: kwhitaker927@gmail.com or kristen.whitaker@dc.gov

Bio: Kristen Whitakers is the only high school teacher to receive the Toyota Teacher of the Year award. As a full time history teacher, Kristen works to engage families of her students through home visits. According to her principal, Maria Tukeva, Kristen has developed family engagement skills that go well beyond the expectations and imagination of the school. Maria shares that, "Through perseverance and continual learning, Kristen devised countless ways of using what she learned about families and students during home visits, to differentiate her classroom teaching."

Runners-up: Donna LaBeaume

Award Year – 2016

JEAN CIBOROWSKI FAHEY

South Shore Hospital, Weymouth, MA

Contact Information: Jean_Fahey@sshosp.org

Bio: Jean Ciborowski Fahey, Ph.D., has been active in the field of early literacy for nearly 40 years. According to Faye Weir, Director of Child Parent Services at South Shore Hospital, Jean designed the South Shore Hospital Reading Partnership to "educate the community about the profound opportunity parents have to build a reading brain in a child's first five years, and thereby prevent many children from experiencing early reading problems." Jean teaches, blogs, and speaks on a variety of early literacy topics, targeting both parents and those who work with parents. Prior to working at South Shore Hospital, Jean assessed young children for reading difficulties at Children's Hospital/Harvard Medical School, worked as an adjunct language and literacy professor at Lesley University, and as an early literacy specialist with the national office of Reach Out and Read. In addition, she held a contract with Massachusetts State Department of Education, Office of Adult Basic Education, where she coordinated family literacy services for Massachusetts' most vulnerable families.

Runners-up: Ellin Klor, Santa Clara, CA

www.ingramcontent.com/pod-product-compliance
Lightning Source LLC
Chambersburg PA
CBHW041548220426
43665CB00003B/61